Penguin Books

THE FORGETTING OF WISDOM

Paul McDermott was born in 1962. He attended art school in Canberra. In 1985 he began writing and performing with The Doug Anthony Allstars. After their demise he spent a few years travelling, returning to Australia in 1995 to work on the television program *Good News Week*.

PAUL McDERMOTT

THE FORGETTING
OF WISDOM

PENGUIN BOOKS

Penguin Books Australia Ltd
487 Maroondah Highway, PO Box 257
Ringwood, Victoria 3134, Australia
Penguin Books Ltd
Harmondsworth, Middlesex, England
Penguin Putnam Inc.
375 Hudson Street, New York, New York 10014, USA
Penguin Books Canada Limited
10 Alcorn Avenue, Toronto, Ontario, Canada M4V 3B2
Penguin Books (NZ) Ltd
Cnr Rosedale and Airborne Roads, Albany, Auckland, New Zealand
Penguin Books (South Africa) (Pty) Ltd
5 Watkins Street, Denver Ext 4, 2094, South Africa
Penguin Books India (P) Ltd
11, Community Centre, Panchsheel Park, New Delhi 110 017, India

First published by Penguin Books Australia Ltd 2000

10 9 8 7 6 5 4 3 2 1

Cover design by David Altheim, Penguin Design Studio
Text design by Erika Budiman, Penguin Design Studio
Author photograph by Michael Amendolia
Typeset in 9.5/14.5 pt Charter by Midland Typesetters, Maryborough, Victoria
Printed and bound by Australian Print Group, Maryborough, Victoria

National Library of Australia
Cataloguing-in-Publication data:

McDermott, Paul, 1962– .
The forgetting of wisdom.

ISBN 0 14 029913 0.

1. Australian wit and humor – 20th century.
I. Title.

A824.3

www.penguin.com.au

For Sparrow, and my dear family

Contents

Acknowledgements

I would like to thank Johannah Fahey for her unfailing kindness, her acute observations and her continual support.

I would also like to thank Andrea Jones at *Sunday Life*, who originally approached me to write for them.

And I would like to thank everyone at the *Australian Magazine* for their patience, especially Rosie Higson.

Finally, thanks to David Altheim for designing the cover for this book.

The Disturbing Introduction

Even in laughter the heart may grieve,
and mirth may end in sorrow.

Proverbs 14:13

Dear Reader

When I first began these columns my primary concern was to communicate truth.

I have tried to be honest, but it's difficult for a person who has been duplicitous for years, who is skilled in deception and has no moral fibre. I have resigned myself to the folly of this initial concept. I am a liar and beg you to accept me as such. Wherever possible I've attempted to remember what I've forgotten. I've taken great care to avoid reality. If some vagary of truth has blocked my path, I've disposed of it thoughtfully. I've avoided focusing on myself, preferring to find fault with others. At all times, I've sought to remain calmly irrational and passionately subjective.

This is not a book of promises: there are no remedies or solutions here. These are merely observations, dissections and lamentations on the world that surrounds us. (At times I thought, nay prayed, my research would have the ability to transform me, but I always returned to this hated shell.) Some of the work collected in this volume sat with me like a curse, loitering in the lobby of my mind refusing to transfer itself to the page. Other stories flew from my fingertips. Some innocently tormented me when I could not find the definitive word or the correct turn of phrase. Some I laboured over, while others seemed to materialise as I slept. Some weighed me down with the intolerance of a 'weekly obligation' and others, when held to the light, brought me a small amount of joy. They're journeys into my temperament, each one coloured by the hour it was written. I have collected them here, the loathed and the loved, under one roof, a book of moods.

I trust that when you hold them to the light, you too will find something of worth.

Paul McDermott
Buenos Aires
August 2000

Concerning Humanity

CONCERNING HUMANITY

Self-Help for the Helpless

• Part 1

There is no doubt that we live in an era of high stress, aggression and abrupt change. Nothing prepares us for the terror of modern life. We are not equipped for the unexpected turns, the betrayals, the lies, the incriminations or even the ennui that binds it all together. Thankfully help is at hand. For every mental, physical and spiritual ailment society hurls at us a book exists to combat it. The message is clear: if you're about to die an emotional death, bury yourself in a book.

Seeking to understand this phenomenon I went in search of a book store. Hoping to find a text that spoke to me, I strolled into an average-looking book store. There was nothing free or freaky about the place. There were no love beads hanging from the ceiling, no smell of frankincense or patchouli oil. Yet the place was a refuge for those in need. They clung to the shelves, crouching in the shadows, designer slacks, credit cards and expensive sunglasses disguising their tears. Every accessory was a testament to the harshness of life. These people were here for one thing and one thing only – self-improvement. The book store should have set up a soup kitchen. It was offering what religion used to offer: that feeling of community, safety, acceptance, the sense that any sin could be forgiven. Yet pews remain empty while book stores thrive, and for one simple reason: how can a pamphlet on heavenly salvation compete with the brutal honesty of *If I'm So Wonderful, Why Am I Still Single*? We need answers, and we need them now. A quick fix, a pat on the back, a shoulder to cry on and someone who understands. Even if that someone is a psychologist with dubious credentials and a grip on reality straight out of Dr Seuss.

It wasn't hard to find what I was looking for. The self-help books took up 80 per cent of the store yet the entire history of the world was confined to two meagre racks. (What sort of world have we created where the knowledge accrued over thousands of years is dwarfed by the output of Southern California?) Books with alluring titles like *Get Out of Your Own Way*, *The Dance of Anger* and *Love Me! Love My Trauma!* called my name from the shelves.[1]

I had a rush of fear, sensing someone was watching me, trying to decide which book I 'needed'. Was I lost without love? Did I love too much? Was I hurting others to hurt myself? Had I found the child within? Could I learn to smile with my brain? I thought ahead to the potentially embarrassing moment of purchase. Twenty people behind me in the line and I'm holding *Men Who Find Themselves Bad Company*. I would suddenly become transparent.

Purchasing any one of these books would make my private pain public. Everyone else in the store was coping, so why wasn't

I? I looked for a book that might help me through this but there was nothing. Fighting the fear, I grabbed the nearest paperback and let it fall open to any page. This is a trick I learnt years ago. I was being receptive to the book, letting it speak to me. It fell open on a blank page with a price sticker. I picked up another – *There's More to Life Than Sex and Money* – and on a quick perusal discovered nothing to support their case. *How to Disagree Without Being Disagreeable*: this one I threw down in disgust because the title annoyed me.

I leafed through another dozen volumes and still nothing really spoke to me. Why couldn't I find anything that appealed to me, something gently affirming like *I'm OK – You're Completely Stuffed*? Thousands of disposable and tasty texts like so many fad diets for a bulimic mind. *It's Not That I Overeat but My Psyche Has a Gland Problem*. These paperbacks were packed to the brim with common sense. They were overflowing with everyday logic and as much thoughtful research as Mills and Boon. It was then I became aware of a greater tragedy. Self-help addicts in search of the perfect life can never stop at one. It begins with the seven stages of grief but pretty soon you've turned to personal growth and before you know it you're discovering past lives – past lives that were invariably more successful because you didn't have self-help books to help you get through them. I suffered a bout of melancholy for the old days when the remedy for any hurt was time. Those words 'give it time' were a virtual mantra when I was a child. They were happier days, when manic depression could be cured by the phrase 'buck up'.

I did leave the store with a book, and I believe I did not compromise my mission. It was by a real doctor, it put a smile on my face, and it made more sense than anything else I had seen. Even the title intrigued me – *Green Eggs and Ham*.

---

1.   Some of the titles in this article do not exist.

Self-Help for the Helpless

• Part 2

I n a coffee shop crowded with cooing couples a gentleman sits stoically by himself. As love-struck partners exchange pet names over turkish bread his face is buried in a book. Sunday morning oozes into Sunday afternoon. He sips his short black, his brow furrowed, his eyes moist with tears. The attention of everyone in the coffee shop becomes fixed on this enigma.

One by one we are sucked into the black hole of his pathos. His fingers are splayed out over the edge of his book. They are tortured hands, bent and twisted. This has less to do with any physiological deformity and more to do with displaying the title. He holds the tome at an awkward angle, facing the busy street.

If one were suspicious one might say he held the book so that anyone or everyone could read that cover: *HOW TO OVER-COME THE HURT AND LEARN TO LOVE AGAIN*. Beneath, in smaller print, it read: *A guide for generous loving men whose lives have been destroyed by the whims of wily women.*

If he had been reading the memoirs of Churchill or the *Debbie Does Dallas* pop-up picture book no-one would have cared. As it was, that book made him seem interesting – not interesting enough for anyone to stay with, but more interesting than without the book. He became a riddle that needed a solution. Who hurt him? Would he overcome the hurt? Would he learn to love again? Why on earth was he reading such tripe in a public place?

Still, there was something intoxicating about the vulnerability of the guy. He was wearing his heart on his sleeve. Not just his heart, but his stomach, his spleen, the desire of his loins: they were all there sitting on his sleeve. Even parts of his brain seemed dangerously exposed by the book he was holding.

A tiny voice deep inside me cried out in sympathy. 'Here's a troubled man who is not afraid to bare his tormented soul to a group of strangers in a coffee shop on a Sunday morning.' Sadly, that tiny voice was completely overpowered by another voice, a voice shouting and hurling abuse: 'This is a manipulative and insidious public display. Here is a blatant attempt by an emotionally scarred trapdoor spider to lure an unsuspecting female fly to its doom.'

'No,' the little voice cried, 'it's just a coincidence that he's sitting facing the street. It's just a coincidence that he's in the prime position, at the largest table, in the only pool of sunlight. It's just a coincidence that due to his position he looks like Ramses the sun god – a slightly balding sun god admittedly, but a sun god nonetheless.'

That book sickened me. With its soothing pastel toning it appeared like any number of generic no-name off-the-shelf self-help books. There was nothing on the cover apart from words, big words. By this I don't mean long words, just words in extra-large type. There was no picture, no thoughtful design, just calming colours and the title screaming out in block letters. The subtext of which was, 'You need me, you stuff-up. Buy me, and I'll make your mundane life bearable.' Beneath the title sat the name of Dr No-One from Nowhere, Southern California. This is not his real name but I certainly don't want to get sued by some crystal-gazing ex-hippie who's all sunshine and love until they see big money in a defamation case. The term 'Dr' shimmered in a rainbow of purity that suggested depth, honesty and whole-some, positive earth vibes. Following the good doctor's name came a list of academic credentials that leapt off the page like a coked-up gerbil.

The day turned cool as evening approached. I had run up a bill of over $100 for tea, orange juice and Turkish bread. Trap-door folded that fabulous book into the warmth of his jacket, making sure to keep the title in plain view. He gave one last mournful look around to see if anyone would take the bait. There were no nibbles. He sauntered off into the gathering dusk. As the street lamps obscured him from view, I wondered, 'What's more pathetic: a man reading a self-help book in a crowded coffee shop, or a man watching a man reading a self-help book in a crowded coffee shop?' I was furious with him as I headed home. What was so fascinating? It wasn't *War and Peace*. Why do there have to be 300 pages plus of life-affirming crap? Here's a solution to the question in two lines. 'How to overcome hurt'? Just get over it! And on the more difficult topic of 'Learning to love again'? Give it a shot! As the night swallowed me I had a vision of his home. There on his bedside table sat another self-help book: *How to Cope with Rejection After a Day of Looking Like a Dill in a Coffee Shop in a Desperate Attempt to Get a Bit of Attention.*[1]

---

1. I'd like to apologise for all this aggression but I have some issues I need to resolve.

An Age-Old Dilemma

This is the Year of the Older Person.[1] So far I have missed the celebrations but they're happening all around us: on cruise ships the Latino strains of the Tijuana Brass are dislocating hips, in rest homes there are orgies of laxatives and sponge baths, and by this bleak September in the 'September of their years' some of our older people will be finding love.

Celebrating the older person is a beautiful idea but there are practical concerns that must be voiced. The first: perhaps the older person has enough to celebrate with the arrival of Viagra. Does the older person really have the heart to celebrate anything else? OPs (older persons) have been telling us for years they're sexual beings, driven by dark animal urges to procreate and forage licentiously. I believe most of society accepts this – we just don't want to think about it too much.

The second dilemma (this may appear callous on the surface, but take a minute to consider it in depth): how many of the goodly, wintry folk are going to make it to the celebrations at the end of the year? I'll warrant a great number of the geriatric funsters who started in January on a high won't be there for the

closing party. It's a terrible thought to have amid all these festiv-
ities, but it's something we must be conscious of. It's all fun now,
but by May the croakers will be a bit teary and looking for a nice
place to lie down. They will have tuckered themselves out by
June and the rest of the year will be spent complaining. August
will see them having an afternoon nap that lasts until October.
And it's best not to think about all the arrangements we'll have
to make in November and December. Thankfully younger people
are becoming older people every day. We may take some solace
in the fact that the end will be just as full of back ailments,
fatigue, dementia and weeping sores as the beginning.

Where young people are dynamic and wild, old people are
sage and wise. The OPs have acquired a lifetime of knowledge,
wisdom and understanding, they have battled for love and
liberty, and they have made fine jams. The marvellous tales the
elderly could tell would keep the no-good drug-addled young
people of today entranced for hours – if the fogies could just
remember them. Most of the time the rebels-of-yesteryear are
sitting two inches away from the TV (I remember, before TV,
what fun we'd have, sitting around a wireless and looking at
it . . .) lusting after the Queen Mum's fashion sense or praising
the straight-down-the-line policies of Pauline.

There's nothing new about the Year of the Older Person,
and there is no time like the present to respect our older citizens, giving them the tributes and kindness they deserve. I, for
one, enjoy the company of the OPs, though I must say, I'm not
that keen on the smell. It is my belief that we should heap praise
on the elderly every year, but not enough to strain their hernias.
The old may not be our most precious resource but we only
have to look at classic films like *On Golden Pond*, *Grumpy Old*

Men and *Soylent Green* to know their real worth. And in the end, if we reach the end, we all get old. Any spindly, glaucoma-ridden creature reading this knows only too well what's waiting for us once we throw up the sweet wine of youth.

I tried, in this article, not to succumb to the stereotypical image of the elderly as petulant, grumpy Monarchists whose only joy is to be a burden to their family. This sort of attitude would be as blinkered as suggesting that all young people are misguided, useless Republicans whose only joy is to be a burden to their family. I failed in this task because I feel bitter and cheated: they've managed to do it again. They've managed, which is more irritating than anything else, to screw up our chance of having a Year of the Older Person when *we* are older people. Once again the previous generation has had their cake and sucked-it-up-with-a-straw too. They had the wars and the sixties, the atomic age and the Beatles, while we got disco, the eighties, AIDS and Kaja Goo Goo. By the time we reach the OP years it'll be the Year of the Young Person again, or the Foetus, or the Unconceived.

It is said that youth and all its trappings (spontaneity, excessive joy, foolishness, wonder) are wasted on the young. This year they belong to the older person. So to all the lucky OPs: celebrate, but watch your backs.

---

1.   The Year of the Older Person was 1999.

Mini Minor Miracles in Melbourne

The wind was whipping along the length of Collins Street leaving in its wake an avenue of brittle leaves. As the evening began I was making my way to dinner, head bowed, determined. It was about this time the first small miracle occurred: the miracle of the angel and the sailor. I was transported to Albert Tucker's view of the forties, but gone were the *Victory Girls* and the pain of war, replaced by a scene of peaceful beauty.

Sitting atop a guardrail beside a tram stop was a woman. She looked resplendent in a full-length blue coat, and from her back, pale-pink lucent wings emerged. The membranes quivered as she craned forward towards a young sailor, their mouths inches apart. As they waited for a tram they almost kissed. It was a magical vision of restrained passion. Along the street trams rattled, igniting the air with electrical sparks. As I turned the corner into Russell Street I confronted the second miracle: the miracle of the contumacious cars.

Two vehicles had approached a single parking space in the middle of Russell Street from opposite sides of the road. Each driver must have seen the opening and, overcome with relief, cruised into the available space. Imagine the overwhelming sense of disappointment when another unseen suitor for the gap nudged their bumper, challenging them for possession. It was a stand-off, a stalemate.

They stood their ground inside their cars, breath frosting on the glass. It was just a matter of time. Eventually one of the combatants would prevail and the other, nursing his wounds, would have to pay for a commercial park somewhere in a well-lit labyrinth of concrete, the perfect park, like the fish that got away, lost to them forever. And as I made my way to dinner, I was impressed by their stubbornness. I applauded their bull-headed stupidity. I enjoyed a pleasant meal, interspersed with hasty conversation, but what happened to me is largely unimportant. When I trudged back up the road an hour later I discovered nothing had changed.

There sat our two protagonists exactly where I had left them. On closer inspection it was clear that this was far more than a mere battle of wills. It was an archetype of confrontation. This was the age-old struggle between father and son, experience and exuberance, age and youth: in one car a young couple, in the other an older man.

The car closest to me was a Mini Minor and it contained the youngsters. The guy might have recently acquired a backbone because of the object of desire who sat beside him. She was his Helen of Troy, his Cleopatra. Empires would fall and car-parking spaces would be won in her name. How could he retreat when he was only the sum total of what she believed him to be? Besides, he was young. He had time on his side. If he waited long enough perhaps the old guy would die.

The other car, which sat diametrically opposed in perfect symmetry with the Mini, was an Australian classic – a rat-arsed copper Fairlane – and visible through the bug-crusted windscreen, a well-worn Aussie face. The driver had a brow so furrowed small creatures could have passed unnoticed between his temples. He had waited all his life for this park and was not about to let it be lost to some dole-bludging show-off with his fancy-dancin' lady friend. After all it was Sunday night in the city and this was the most fun he could have. He could wait. He could wait forever.

This was not road rage, it was passive-aggressive parking, auto-antagonism. In America someone would already have been shot. And what thoughts were tumbling through their heads? If only I had left home a minute earlier. If only I had driven faster. If only I had an eighteen-wheeled monster truck to push that miserable dung heap into the oncoming traffic. If only I had a gun.

It was clear this clash of titans was here for the long haul: from the Mini I could hear the dismal sounds of Steps; in the Fairlane Jerry Vale was in mid-croon. I had to leave.

I would like to believe they are still there, adhered to the moist Melbourne road, belligerently battling on, with a small crowd of onlookers feasting like vultures on the dumb display. Concerned people would be bringing food, welfare agencies dropping off blankets, and the continued inaction splitting society down the middle. Brawls in pubs, and heated coffee shop conversations: 'Are you for the Ford or the Mini?' If only it had been a Holden it would have been exquisite. And in years to come a shrine would be erected to the 'Miracle of Russell Street', a small memorial plaque and a bronze statue of two men with the combined brain power of Greyfriars Bobby – two men who wasted away their lives in their bucket seats.

Elsewhere life had moved on. The sailor and the girl with angel wings had caught a tram and disappeared into the all-consuming Melbourne night. That was how the evening ended: two miracles without a moral.

Anzac Day 1999

In Praise of Tea

The Australian tea ceremony ranks as one of the truly beautiful antipodean traditions. Even when there is no food in the cupboard a family can be brought together around the pot. When this society, bitter with rage, disheartened by the transience of political promises, baffled by the current state of affairs and doomed to repeat the mistakes of its forebears, sits down and has a cuppa char, suddenly, silently, all is right with the world. This humble leaf is the gateway to truth. It transforms into a brilliantly scalding brew that can burn lies off the roof of the mouth. As the 'teatotalling' poet once said, 'In Camellia sinensis veritas.'

There is nothing more seductive than the early-morning brew. The first sip brings with it a measure of warmth, understanding and purity that can only be imagined when one drinks other legal beverages. It's the truck driver's friend, the housewife's companion, so heavy with tannin it'd rip the enamel off your back teeth. We are the first among the great tea-drinking nations of the world. Our tea ceremony has an earthy honesty about it. It is a ceremony that doesn't stand on ceremony. There is nothing like a decent cuppa to resurrect the heart of the downtrodden, give strength to the weak and find the lost. Yet the meek divinity of the Aussie tea ceremony is under threat.

Look at the coffee-slurping multitudes with crusts of foam solidifying on their upper lips. Is there anything more disturbing in the early hours of the morning than finding an acquaintance who's brown-nosed a mocha? Or bent the ear of a waiter until it's bleeding with countless infantile instructions on how to construct their morning pick-me-up? It's this desperate need to be noticed that has resulted in thousands of variants of the bean-based libation. Does a taste that truly satisfies continue to elude these devotees of the *Coffea arabica*? Where has their torrid search left them? With agitated limbs, blood-rimmed eyes lurching from the skull on nebulous stalks, and talking nonsense until the shaking stops. Consider now the drinker of tea: restrained, contemplative, and sure of their place in the world. Tea has always had a spiritual basis while coffee has merely greased the wheels of industry.

Coffee houses sprang up in the 17th century as centres for business. In Europe they were formed in conjunction with insurance companies as a way of seducing customers. In New York's Merchant's coffee house treason was discussed.[1] Coffee continues to fuel business to this day. The tedious habits of the addicted coffee consumer have been mocked and ridiculed to such a degree that I believe there is nothing constructive I can add. Suffice to say that in the inner city the ordering of coffee is as emotionally deadly, and as fraught with danger, as a descent into the circles of hell.

And yet coffee is not the only enemy. Today tea is also under fire from a diverse range of supposedly healthy, life-style-enhancing, spiritually robust herbal substitutes. Trading on the illustrious history of the one true leaf these pretenders to the crown, these usurpers, claim to cure every ailment from acne to xenophobia. They're sealed in designer boxes and are available in the 'better stores'. They're festooned with pithy comments, justifications and copious notes on their application or digestion. They're alchemic combinations of dried flower stems and over-zealously pulped fruits, and they have the taste of watered-down incense. It's as if someone has gone through the mulch, picked out the least offensive rotted tree roots, and poured boiling water over them. If nature had a bowel this is the sort of crap that would collect in cancerous pools along the alimentary canal. To harvest it, to seal it in a flow-throw bag, to call it 'tea', is an anathema to all real tea drinkers.

In the East it's suggested the first teapot was formed by Bodhidharma's eyelids. He removed them to stop him falling asleep while he was meditating. Here in the West tea is just as rich with religious resonance. Its common form in this country has three equally powerful components, and thus mirrors the unity and diversity of the Holy Trinity: tea, water (the eternal life force) and full-fat milk (life is too short to skim). As St Thomas Aquinas completed his glorious argument for the existence of God, the 'five ways', he is said to have cried, 'All life, thought and excellence flows from the spout.'

A decent cup of tea, white or black, can soothe all society's ills, real or imagined. There's no need for sticks and twigs claimed to be panaceas for the spiritually deficient or the jittery caffeine-induced panic of the latte drinker. In this life let us always thirst for the truth, and in that thirst let us be sustained by tea.

---

1. Would this great nation be any wiser had they not dumped hundreds of boxes of tea (the beverage of the civilised, the bringer of peace that leads, through devotion, to the elimination of the ego, and yet symbol of their oppression) into Boston Harbor?

On Insomnia

On my return to work I decided to clean out my desk. There, stuffed in the drawers, were the collected ravings of '97: hastily jotted notes, unfinished thoughts and diary entries for things I had forgotten to do. In the middle of the mess I found a curious pile of handwritten papers. I went to throw them out but the style of writing intrigued me. I had never seen anything like it before. It was almost illegible, completed in a childlike scrawl with numerous scribbles and scratches. Small drawings of severed heads filled the margin, and here and there the ink had been smudged by tears. It took me a while to realise that I had written it myself.

To help you understand this situation I should give you some background briefing. During 1997 I was co-presenting a breakfast radio program. At the time I was rising for work about 5 a.m. Due to my other commitments I wasn't arriving home until around 7 or 8 p.m. This might not have been a bad thing had I been able to go to bed at that time, but there is something tragic about a grown man going to bed before children and I just couldn't do it. I tried once or twice but I'd end up just lying there getting angrier and angrier as I watched the hours tick by. I was surviving on less than four hours' sleep a night, which was fine under normal circumstances. (On the up side, I'm usually very irritable and grumpy and now had a good excuse for my moods.) The problem arose when I stopped sleeping altogether – when bed became the part of the day when I lay still for a few hours and stared at the ceiling. Around this time I went a little mad. Below is a transcription of the papers I found.

Ask not for whom the bell tolls, it tolls for thee. What's the use of setting the alarm if you're always awake? How many times can you check a watch in a minute?

Sheep. Last night I counted them, thousands of them, jumping over fences. Well, they started jumping, but that was a bit strenu-ous. Pretty soon they were bumming fags, standing around the fence or hitching lifts out of my dream. After 200 I was very bored with the whole 'jumping sheep' concept. At about 320 they began to lose body parts to the abattoir. By 480 armies of handicapped ghost sheep appeared. By 660 only bloodless limbs and skinned heads were being tossed over the fence. A pile of offal collected at the base of my dream. I am looking forward to 'sleep' tonight – perhaps I will graduate to cows or even humans.

I am not complaining.[1] I am fully aware that there are those citizens whose burden is greater than mine. This does not, however, prevent me from dwelling on the injustices I suffer in my own life, the most recent of which is a disturbing bout of insomnia. I say 'bout' in absolute certainty that it is not a permanent affliction. It is a phase I am going through, a troubled period that with time will evaporate leaving the path to sleep once more open to me. HELP.

Presently I have the appearance of a derelict – a derailed human being, a lifeless Tamagotchi. I have become the social equivalent of Mir: malfunctioning, uncaring, self-destructive and heading to God knows where. I have tried a vast number of concoctions designed to knock me out. Helpful hippies from all over the country (mainly Mullumbimby) have sent truckloads of herbal remedies: sickening potpourri from their bush gardens, evil alchemical recipes of a foul-tasting nature. One bag was filled with what I believe was illegal drugs. Do these people think that to cure my insomnia I would break the law? Thankfully, a cleaner offered to dispose of the stuff. He referred to these people as 'wicked' and kept saying, 'Evil man, sending a whole bag of heads.'

How can anything herbal help in this battle against the self? I need something synthetic, hard core, something developed on the banks of the Rhine, something that has millions of dollars and hundreds of hours of research put into it. I need something I can buy in a tamper-proof airtight foil container. Something I can swallow with water. Something from the chemist.

A pharmacist was kind enough to prescribe a legal sedative that doubles as an animal tranquilliser. He claimed just one of these innocent-looking capsules could knock over a rhino. I was game and took a couple. By 4 a.m. my entire body was comatose, apart from my eyes, which were wired to the ceiling. I wanted to be home on the Serengeti. 'God damn, those sheep are moving slow. Perhaps it's because they don't have any legs. No! They're floating. Gravity-defying sheep – if Mir had them strapped to the solar panels it'd never come down. Is that the alarm? I didn't set the alarm. Why set the alarm if you're always awake?'

---

1.   Of course I'm complaining.

The Wisdom of the Ages

A pub is the perfect place for gambling. In fact anywhere with a bar would be perfect. That edge of nervousness, oft accompanied by risking one's life savings, can be dulled by the constant and varied application of alcoholic beverages.

I was lured into the bar by the aged. What were they doing here? What did they know that we didn't? What had seventy-odd years of joy and sorrow taught them? Was this where the accumulated knowledge of a lifetime had led them? Was this what their wisdom, like some long-dormant instinct, had demanded of them?: that they sit on high stools for hours, riding the one flat shandy, pumping machines they claim are 'theirs'? We have so much to learn from the older members of our community. I wanted to learn why they loved the pokies.

I found a quiet corner of the bar. *Elf Forest, Golden Apples, Big Safari, Mighty Pyramids, Jungle Adventure.* No wonder the old ones were packed like sardines. It was like a Johnny Weiss-muller film festival. I settled on a pokie emblazoned with lions but I felt uncertain, even slightly dirty, as I smoothed my plastic money and slid it into the slot. (My only previous gamble had been with religion. It was the standard bet: a life of moral servitude and faithful adherence to the laws of the church for a crack at eternal life. I'm still waiting on the outcome.) At first my machine was reluctant to take the cash. It spat it back out with a groan. Maybe it was a decent bandit? Maybe it was giving me the option to walk away? I pushed again, and this time it accepted my donation. That was when the world changed. Just by putting the money in the machine I had leapt from a measly $20 to a phenomenal 2000 one-cent credits. I was already ahead. Maybe there was more to this than I thought.

The barrels began spinning with dizzy enthusiasm, taunting me with a two of a kind before granting me a small victory. With that minor win came the melody – the little song the machine sings to let everyone know you have won the battle of wills. But the machine is a relentless tempter. It tempts with the first bet, the amount you bet and the number of lines you bet on. When you finally win it tempts you with double or nothing, half-stake, spin again. It stretches the wealth of the world before you and asks you to choose red or black. And again. And again.

Gambling is emotionally addictive. They should take those cancer-ridden rodents off the shit-sticks and give them a turn on the pokies. At every touch of the button you embark on a roller-coaster ride of emotions: the giddy high when the uplifting chorus of chimes indicates that you're a master of the buttons; the humiliating silence when lady luck turns her back and slinks off with some other punter. Between the histrionics and the heart attacks, the crinklies are having a ball.

I had believed pokies were a blight – mechanical maggots; money-milking machines. They transformed user-friendly pubs into inhospitable mini-Vegas landscapes. They were responsible for the destruction of the local music scene. They created monsters within families. But when my machine sang her little song, when I witnessed five scattered zebras with two pixilated eagles flying on a 50 cent bet over ten lines, I found I could forgive them everything. There on the credit counter was my dream numeral: 200 000.

Even as I watched my instant wealth drain away I found it hard to harbour any feelings of mistrust towards them. Although it did cause me to cry out in a loud voice, 'Father, Father, why hast thou abandoned me?' In the happy midafternoon bar-room limbo no-one turned their head. This sort of pathetic petition to the heavens must have been made all too frequently. With a feeling of resignation I was aware I had reached our new century, my starting point, on the 1 cent credit counter. I found myself falling backwards through time. 2000, 1985, 1935, 1900, 1815. It took mere seconds for me to reach the Age of Reason, bypass it and fall headlong into the Dark Ages. And still the credit counter fell: 800, 750, 700. Eventually I was down to a 1 cent bet on one line. If I lost this I'd be present at the birth of our Lord, year dot, nothing left in the bank. The electronic barrel turned and then there was silence.

The pokies may be pure evil, but when everything turns against you, then here, sheltered from the roar of the world, you're capable of glorious, if momentary, victories. Today I could walk away, but there will come a time, when I'm older and wiser, when the shandies are cheap and it's happy hour in purgatory, and then I'll stay. I'll stay to hear the song of the machines.

On Public Displays
of Affection

There are some days you wake to find yourself out of step with the rest of the world. When an incident or circumstance places you in opposition to all around you. When you are forced to ask, 'Is it me or is the world mad?'

Last Sunday I entered a small, crowded cafe, and although it was 4 p.m., to me it felt like 7 a.m. (something to do with a late night and several missing hours). I needed a pot of tea and some food to rejoin the land of the living. What I craved was something to nourish my flesh. What I received was something that sapped my soul.

A couple were sitting at a table just in front of me, and as I sat down they started to kiss. They kissed long and they kissed hard and there were tongues involved. This was not an affectionate dry kiss; this was a loud, wet public display of sexuality. I tried to look away, but I felt awkward and self-conscious staring at the ceiling. I buried my head in the paper, but my eyes kept being dragged back to the spectacle before me.

The waitress took my order. This was my world too. Why should I be embarrassed by their behaviour? Why should I look somewhere else? I couldn't avoid it: I surrendered and decided to stare. By the time my food arrived they had still not come up for air.

They broke their mouth grip and I breathed a sigh of relief. Another couple of minutes and I'm sure one of them would have died. Unexpectedly something more nauseatingly saccharine than the kiss occurred: the meaningful stare. An inch apart they gazed into each other's eyes with a fevered intensity. In this way they avoided the pock-marked skin, sagging jowls and greasy hair of their partner and fell headlong into the iris. Their eyes remained locked together, their hands roamed freely, and then guess what happened? They kissed again.

It was like watching a car crash in slow motion, their faces colliding and absorbing the impact of each other, their tongues lolling obscenely out of their heads, their noses twisting and collapsing into their cheeks. This visual aspect was hideous enough, but it was the aural dimension that managed to put me off my breakfast. They pulled apart with a slobbering smack, leaving their mouths glistening with saliva. I struggled to keep down the food I hadn't eaten. It was an ugly, vulgar sound, animalistic and all too human, reminding me that we were no better than the beasts in the field.

I wasn't the only voyeur – everyone was watching the show. This was their moment, a moment that had lasted over an hour. (And it wasn't only the moment that bothered me – it was what had occurred before and would occur after the moment. My imagination was running rampant. What had led them to this, and where would this lead them? Did they need these prying eyes to 'get off'? Would there be any point if no-one was watching? When they got home would they go into separate rooms

exhausted by their 'meal'? Did they have nothing to talk about?)
Another couple moved to a closer table to get a better view.

The nose-breathing lovers had put me off my breakfast, but
it must have caused a mighty appetite in them because they
jumped straight into their tucker. It gave us our second rest; this
time the entire cafe was relieved, but it didn't last long. Unper-
turbed by the egg and Kransky sausage half-masticated in his
mouth she tore in for another kiss. She slammed her face into
his, open-mouthed and panting. I'm not sure what she was
eating, but after that, he would've had a fair idea. Kissing,
chewing, chewing, kissing and, now, drinking and kissing. I
prayed a hot coffee would cool their ardour, but they downed
their lattes and, frothing at the mouth, resumed the tongue
lashing.

I was confident my fellow diners would be equally disgusted
but the opposite was true. The exhibitionists had a sickening
lovey-dovey domino effect on the other patrons. Every other
couple (I was the only lone diner) in the place began to coo to
each other. It was as if they were given permission to be amorous
by the excessive display they'd seen. People were laughing,
giggling, stroking each other's thighs. The whole place was
canoodling; even the rational waiters and cooks were engaged
in a bit of frottage. It was disgusting, and I realised I didn't belong
there. Maybe there was something in the coffee? Had some
pagan deity sprinkled fairy dust in the food? Was I the only Jesuit
at a bacchanalian festival?

I left my untouched breakfast and undrunk tea and returned
to the safety of my home. This was a day when opinion had
turned against me, and I found myself alone. I had been made
all too aware of my solitude, not just within the coffee shop but

within the world at large. These two people, who were desperately trying to be one, had left me feeling incredibly divided. I went back to bed; I have no idea if they did.

Radical Approaches to
Gender Roles

I t came from California, a dynamic new concept in human
relations. It came as a word whispered by inspired youth
who challenged the status quo. It was driven by the need
for the sexes to unite in something more than the base coupling
required for procreation. It called for the barriers developed over
centuries of systematic, enforced sexual repression to disappear.
It demanded the sexes become indistinguishable. It promised a
liberated sexual democracy, a brave new republic. It was a word
that would change the way that men and women related: unisex.

It is a word that many will remember, although it has all but
been erased from our language. The old guard saw 'unisex' as
something dangerous, but to the young it was a call to arms. Like
freedom or liberty, the mere mention of the word caused governments to tremble. It spread like wildfire through populations
eager for revolution. For men and women tired of the seemingly
arbitrary roles society imposed, here was a concept that would
render them obsolete.

Virtually overnight unisex clothes, bars, clubs, coffee shops
and tobacconists sprang up. Suddenly men and women could

mingle, share ideas, hopes and dreams. A few older establish-
ments held out against this tidal wave of change, they paid the
price for their stoicism: their numbers dwindled and within a
few years they no longer existed. There was nothing on the face
of the earth that couldn't become unisex. To make anything
gender specific was a crime against nature. Humanity had come
of age, proudly proclaiming its individuality by celebrating
its sameness. Fabrics that had previously been the preserve of
women became popular with men: gabardine, organza, polyes-
ter, velveteen, corduroy and Glo-mesh. Pastimes from the male
domain, like steer-riding and spitting, attracted women. Women
stood proudly by their brothers in pants suits. Without fear of
embarrassment or workplace ridicule, men could wear Bonnie
Bell strawberry-flavoured lipgloss, cruise to the office in their
roller-shoes and sport chunky zodiac jewellery.

This dark horse escaped the doomed utopian vision of the
sixties and forced its way into the seventies. It was in this age of
hedonism and wild abandon that it flourished, and as a child, it
was here I first encountered it.

After the strict confines of my upbringing it was initially
disturbing to witness men and women conversing in public
places. Nothing will compare with the shock I felt entering my
first unisex toilet.[1] The confusing genderless image on the door
opened my eyes to a world of tiled wonder. I was filled with a
mixture of horror and excitement when I heard conversations
from both sexes rising from the cubicles. It may have been
nothing more than a request for paper, but who knows where
that might have led, empires have fallen with less.

It was in Raymond's Swinging Unisex Salon that I observed
the true merits of unisex culture. Here 'man' and 'wo-man' could

sit side by side and have a haircut, blow-dry and rinse. Men could get their hair crimped, shagged, tinted or flicked while women settled for a trim and shave and neither felt self-conscious. Both genders chortled as they leafed through *Pix People* or wept openly at another tragedy in *Woman's Day*. *Californian Poppy* mixed with the chemical scent of *Gossamer Hair* as they discussed politics and art beneath enormous pale-blue egg-shaped dryers. As Raymond's hairy knuckles created a universe of androgynous styles the world changed for me.

Here was a period of unsurpassed creativity and design. There is often regret and embarrassment over post-sixties, pre-eighties fashion. I believe this has more to do with the fact that we, as a people, are ashamed we let such a vibrant and unrestrained period pass us by. The Renaissance pales beside the explosion of thought that accompanied the unisex movement. (Let us never forget this was the period that gave us body language.) We weren't ready for the seventies. Perhaps we never will be. It is only now, twenty years later, that we can begin to appreciate the immense service this decade performed for civilisation.

The haircuts have long since fallen out of favour, just as the clothing has gone out of vogue, but the fervour and lust for life I perceived will always be in fashion.

---

1. There is a tendency in the male to combine the act of urination with the breaking of wind. This display of territorial barbarism disappeared with the advent of the unisex convenience. A new etiquette arose: men became gentlemen and would almost never engage in this sort of behaviour if a woman was present. If they did they would apologise for their vulgarity rather than laugh and proclaim loudly, as they tended to do in purely male environments, 'Better out than in.'

Division in the Family

[concerning custody of the Sunday paper]

There comes a time when, as a people, we must be divided. It is in these times of division that we can more fully understand our character, that we can grow and mature. It is important that we come to understand our differences and implement the changes needed to create a better society. There is an ever-widening gap in this bountiful country, a gap between those who have and those who have not, a gap between the givers and the takers, a gap between those who use and those who are used. I am aware that I am addressing two radically different groups of people, and it is essential that you discover which category you belong to.

To enable you to do this we have designed a simple questionnaire. Please choose either (a) or (b) below.

(a) I have purchased my newspaper, with its numerous sections, colour supplements and special lift-outs, with my hard-earned cash made from the sweat of my brow and the work of my hands.

(b) I have grabbed/found/stolen/borrowed my newspaper (or bits

of it, the aforementioned newspaper) from my husband/wife/
spouse/friend/family member; I have no intention of paying
for it in any way.

If you answered (a), you are entitled to read the paper at
your leisure, to savour the entertainment, envy the lively intellectual debates and skim the personals. It's the right of ownership, and you may exercise it as you will for you are a valued
member of society.

If you answered (b) a sense of shame and debasement
should settle on you as you read. You are a parasite, surviving
on the kind, magnanimous nature of your host.

Every time a paper is 'shared' valuable revenue is lost. The
country as a whole suffers as a result of the greed of a stingy
few. The average adult spends $4 on the weekend papers. A
measly $4 a week that over the course of a year will exceed $200.
If we multiply this figure by a standard lifetime you're looking
at an investment of around $15 000. I remind you that this sum
is derived from the consumption of the weekend papers alone;
one can only imagine the loss if you're buying a paper every day
and someone else is reading it. A mouse might only nibble at a
cake but over time it can consume everything.

The reason the Sunday papers were forced to print more
sections was to create harmony within the home. (It was not, as
some scurrilous sections of the community have suggested, to
sell more advertising space.) This was a noble idea of the altruistic newspaper magnates and might have succeeded had it not
been for the mean-spirited, vicious, uncompromising greed of
the common people. A greater selection of sections only meant
more to fight over, and in these disputes ownership was

irrelevant, possession being ten-tenths of the law.

Individuals are not the only problem. Hotels, hairdressers, gentlemen's clubs, libraries and numerous other businesses diminish the financial return and compromise the integrity of the newspapers. But by far the main offenders are coffee shops. They scatter newspapers and magazines like cerebral cushions to be picked up or discarded by their latte-lapping clientele. For a pitifully small outlay these businesses can impress their customers with the work of others while their customers can compensate them by spending a cowardly dollar or two on a coffee.

There are ways we can stop this terrible downward economic and social spiral: never leave a paper behind on any form of transport, expect family members to buy their own copies and destroy the paper completely when you have finished with it. A newspaper never ends its journey when it leaves your hands. After you finish your rag, you might toss it in a bin. It may be rescued from the bin and casually perused by the garbage man doing the rounds. In the winter months it could be used by a vagrant as a blanket. You may end up paying for it again, as a hidden cost when you purchase fish and chips. Even insects and small animals have been known to use scraps as flotation devices to flee hurricanes. Every man, woman, child, animal and insect under the sun is taking advantage of your largess.

Ask yourself who bought the paper today and who is reading it. Are you sitting sipping tea pretending to be interested in this banal article in another facile magazine supplement while the section you crave is in the hands of someone else? Someone who ruins the articles you intend to read? Someone who's a 'Sunday reader', not a dedicated follower of the news? Someone who never looked at a paper before colour lift-outs? Is there ever a section that mysteriously disappears? Let us not mince words: this 'someone' is the thief who didn't buy the paper in the first place.

Look at them as they happily flick through the pages you own without a care in the world. That physical abyss is hogging the stories you want to read. Is it taking all your strength not to rip it from their ungrateful paws? Hands blackened by newsprint, symbolically tarnished by what they've read, they're an unconscious viper, a drain on all your resources. Take back your paper – you paid for it.

In this article I have taken care to address the owner of the paper. Now I address those of you who chose (b): next week, liberate your wallets or your purses and buy the paper yourself, you miserable lumps of human detritus.

Beach Etiquette

Although it pains me to the core to discuss such a pedestrian topic, the events of recent days have forced my hand. There comes a time to address the commonplace and that time is now. We must clean up our beaches. Not the environmental dilemmas, although they must be addressed – we must clean up our act on the beaches.

We generally exist on the fringe of this country, where the earth frays into the water. Most of the populace avoids the wide, brown land favouring instead the girt-by-sea bit. Australia is composed of lethargic mounds of human beings clustered around inlets of salt water. More than any other nationality, we are of the sea. It is reflected in every aspect of our culture. We are promoted across the globe as a nation of blond-haired, blue-eyed surfer boys and girls who spend endless summers rubbing tanning butter into our young, lithe bodies.

In fact the opposite is true and one trip to the beach will confirm this. Disturbing the pure white sand is a multitude of different-coloured bodies from all over the world, all surviving under a bitterly hot sky. And it is here that as a nation, currently divided, we are truly one. It doesn't matter what faith we profess, our sexual preference or if we have a job, sooner or later we all end up at the beach.

Many of the residents in this country were cheap imports from Britain and Europe. This makes the bulk of us the sworn enemy of daylight. We are genetically predisposed to working down a mine or in a forge under rumbling grey skies. We were never meant for the 'lucky country' with its ludicrous abundance of good things. As summer approaches, our mole-like nature forces us to squirm deeper into the soft, cloying earth. Then on one stinking Sunday we'll leave our burrows and flood to the ocean. When we do venture to the beach we are like fish out of water. This may be the reason that many of us have no idea of beach etiquette. We hit the sand and all sense of decorum leaves us. We become animals, scrounging for towel space, fighting for shade, literally kicking sand in each other's faces.

The experiences below come from half an hour at a popular Sydney beach.

It began with an old gent suffering dementia from the heat, in a saggy pair of lollibags. A weakness in the elastic enabled one hirsute egg to escape as he bent over, his hitherto hidden spud making an unwelcome appearance on the beach. The moment might have passed unnoticed had not a group of young mothers screamed and covered their children's eyes.

Next came the swearing. I'm not proud to say it but I'm au fait with the language of the street, the colourful slang and abusive terminology that dominates American movies and has infiltrated our society. Many would disagree with me but I believe there are occasions that demand excessive verbal aggression. I don't believe Sunday afternoon at the beach is one of them.

Four boys, having survived a torturous puberty, their faces bearing the ritual scars of their passage, stood in front of the young mothers swearing like troopers. Vulgarities tend to jar against the restless wonder of nature. The mothers covered the ears of their offspring. Grabbing a football, the boys began to wrestle each other. Their display of manliness was noticed by everyone they fell on top of. Having destroyed the calm, they soldiered off – as one of them put it, 'to piss in the water'.

Meanwhile two swarthy athletes, their buttocks glistening with sweat and baby oil, pranced about playing paddle ball. The thong is designed for the foot, where it makes a certain amount of practical sense. I'd suggest a turn or two in front of the mirror if you decide to wear this article as beach apparel. It's freeing to be beyond the dictates of fashion and common sense – but a little bit of mystery can be a good thing.

A young mother returned to her brood with some rapidly thawing ice-cream treats. They immediately melted and fell in the sand. The children, much to their mother's disgust, ate them anyway. Flies swarmed around the ice-cream and grit caked on the kids' lips. The mothers squawked like gulls, swatted at the insects and covered the mouths of their howling children.

Over the summer a great deal of our time is spent at the beach. It is important to observe manners, courtesy and good grace even if you are only dressed in semitransparent goolie huggers and thongs. We see a great deal of each other on the beach in summer – perhaps a little too much. Let us strive to expose the best and burn together under the sun.

Attention-Seeking Device

(ASD)

How we cherish those moments when we were the first. When as a child there was wild acclaim and adulation for our simplest actions. Where stumbling forward was rewarded with a kiss. We remember fondly when we were the centre of the universe and all the planets and suns and moons were forced to revolve around us. Over the years the interest generated by that initial appearance dwindles and fades. It dwindles from the eyes of our parents, from the hands of our friends and from the hearts of our loved ones. We are, of course, loved as much as in that first moment but we're just not as interesting. Over time we become commonplace, accepted, nothing special – part of the furniture. Eventually we pass from day to day largely ignored. The ego is affected profoundly by this lack of recognition and as a result invents a multitude of devices that can alleviate the pressure of going through life unnoticed. They're called Attention-Seeking Devices, or ASDs.

My most recent experience of a blatant ASD occurred during the film *Saving Private Ryan*. Several million dollars' worth of investment were totally overpowered by a shallow coughing

device that could have been overcome with a minimal investment in a pack of Throaties. The invasive bacteria assaulting her
lungs were having their own beachhead in her throat. To maintain a sonic dominance over the film the sufferer cleverly
combined her hacking dry cough with a high-pitched 'whisper'.
Thus, between her barking mortar blasts and the untuned static
of her speech, there was always something to drag you back to
her. Tom Hanks could've been marching through Normandy
naked and no-one would have noticed. As she left the cinema
she gladly soaked up the angry glances of the other patrons. A
smug, self-satisfied smile creased her face and she didn't cough
once. It didn't matter that most of them wanted to throttle
her, because in the battle for an audience, she had defeated
Spielberg.

Anthropologists now believe the ASD is as important for our
development as the opposable thumb. If you look around you'll
find that most things we do, don't have to be done at all. Work,
play, sport, philosophy, reproduction: these are merely different
ways to be noticed, of drawing attention to oneself.

A classic ASD that has spanned centuries is the newborn
baby. The question that must be asked is whether this bundle of
joy is the perfect embodiment of the physical union of man and
woman, a testament of love, or an eight-pound Barbie doll made
out of skin. There is enough material in this topic to fill a book
so it's best only to touch on it here. Suffice to say that new
parents are worse than drug dealers when it comes to getting
the unconverted hooked. Any recent convert to the wonders of
reproduction will chant the birth mantra: you've got to have one,
it'll change your life, I've never been so happy. The propagation
of the species is there to have something to speak about.

One popular male trait, which rivals the dance of the rifle-bird for its audacity and shamelessness, is the ability to lose commonplace items. It may be a pair of glasses, a screwdriver or a book put down minutes before that suddenly disappears into the ether. The things that go missing are small everyday objects. It's rare for the fridge or the TV to be lost. A clever ASD sufferer will often incorporate the missing item with a time constraint. It will come as no surprise that the hunt for the car keys comes just prior to leaving the home (e.g. 'I'm late, I'm late – where did I leave those keys?'). The male will insist on searching with unnecessary displays of frustration and annoyance. The reason for this is purely evolutionary: it's an act to attract the partner. Whoever is around is forced to participate in the hunt. The object is frequently in full view, neither misplaced nor gone, but exactly where it should be. This is not the first clumsy step towards senile dementia; it's deeply tied to the human need to create something to talk about, and that something should be oneself. In his awkwardness and disproportionate rage, the male unconsciously affirms his need for a partner while simultaneously attracting much-needed attention to himself. So next time the remote goes missing, remember; it's nothing more than a cry for love.

The true dilemma posed by the ASD epidemic is the domino effect it creates. Once you're aware of the disease it forces you to reassess all your actions and thoughts in light of an 'attention deficiency'. You may create a black hole of self-doubt and descend in a maelstrom of conflict and confusion. There's a simple solution: you're okay if you leave the cinema and you're still coughing or if you find the remote and there's actually something to watch. Use the ASD; never let it use you.

Concerning
Gods

CONCERNING GODS

The New Gods

• Part 1

S cience and religion have always been strange bedfellows. Over the centuries they have been as close as lovers, as distant as bitter enemies. They have often looked in opposite directions to find they shared the same point of view. Occasionally they lie back, light up, and congratulate each other. This happened recently when a scientist discovered the 'God Spot', a part of our brain that sparks with electrical energy whenever the name of God is mentioned.

Every society has had its gods, often the more the merrier. It made a lot of sense to have a different god for every different thing: a god for water, fire, earth, sunflowers, cats. You wanted victory in war, you prayed to Mars; a good harvest, you sacrificed a virgin. The gods drank, ate, defecated and had fascinating sexual relationships. They were uncomplicated gods – greedy, earthy, human. They lacked the psychological complexity and altruism of the later gods. They were in it for the short-term fun, and humanity knew it.

One of the major problems with monotheism is that because a god has to have so many different emotions they end up appearing schizophrenic. 'He is a loving God, and He cares for all his children, apart from those He smites with a plague of toads or burns for eternity in fires of sulfur.' Even our own much-loved Christian god has more personalities than a Street's Two-in-One.

In this day and age of high stress and constant pressure, we need our faith to strengthen us. We have not lost our urge to create gods. They abound as never before. The 'God Spot' is as active as ever. We require new gods, and these new gods deserve our respect and recognition.

Like the old gods, they are small-minded and petty, and couldn't care less about eternal struggles between good and evil. We invoke them whenever we call on them for help.

I lived in a flat where we would call upon the God of Hot Water. 'Please, God, let there be a few minutes of heat before I freeze.' The God of Hot Water always seemed to be deaf until we made a monetary sacrifice to one of his high priests, a plumber called Ron. There is the God of the Radio, who can torment or tantalise. The God of Let The Take-Away Be Open. We ask the God of the Car Park to find a space for us at the crowded shopping mall. For the little God of Money to plant coins at the back of the couch. For the God of the Street to leave something good in the skip. For the God of Washing to return the other sock. For the God of the Bank to make the Biro work. For the God of Sleeping In On Sunday Morning to stop that person playing the French horn.

Some gods seek to make life more difficult for their own delight. These are playful, fickle gods from the line of Loki, Norse God of Mischief. Praying to them is a waste of time. A bloody sacrifice is the only way to gain their attention. Every morning and evening we cram ourselves into their moving cathedrals. We mere mortals are their playthings, clumsy lumps of dough in desperate need of their assistance. It is only by accepting them into our lives that we can reach our final destination. They are the Gods of Transport, a triumvirate of minor deities who wreak havoc with our fragile faith in the written word of the timetable. They are, in order of cruelty, the God of the Bus, the God of the Train and the God of the Cab. I am forced to believe the Gods of Transport exist. The only other conclusion one can reach is too devastating, too frightening: with malice aforethought transport services are conspiring to make our lives a living hell.

What little prayer do you murmur after a long day at work? If you are like me you pray to the Television God. 'Please let there be something good on the TV – Oh God, let there be something good.' And is there something good? NO! There's never anything good. And why not? Because the Television God does not exist. We invented him. We created the Television God to fill an unhappy void in our lives. The Television God doesn't exist, so it does you no service to pray to him. You've got to pray to the God of Programming. And the God of Programming is the most self-important, talentless, middle-of-the-road, arse-licking glorified accountant the universe ever had the displeasure to fart into existence.

After all this talk of God, your 'God Spot' should be hyperactive. Electrical energy should be pulsing in that section of your brain that believes in a higher authority, a greater force in the universe. Did some celestial being place it there or did it develop as a way of ordering society? No doubt science and religion will battle it out again to find another answer that leads to yet another question.

The New Gods

• Part 2

[the Street God]

As we have already seen, we live in a world surrounded by gods. There are the gods of all the major religions, the gods of the lesser religions and finally the deities that we create for our own pleasure. One such deity is the God of the Street.

- Where other gods ask for a life lived in chastity, the Street God only requires that you have a keen eye.
- Where other gods ask for a life of servitude, the Street God asks for patience and perseverance.
- Where other gods look for the good inside, the God of the Street leaves the good outside. He leaves the good in plain view where His followers discover it.
- Once the good is discovered it can be reshaped, refashioned, reborn.
- A spoiled recliner from a North Shore home becomes a cosy reading chair in a Newtown squat, discarded bricks become a bookshelf, an old sign a novel highlight above a Mancare bar.

- The Street God is seldom recognised by the rich. He belongs to the poor.
- His temples are garbage bins and anywhere refuse collects. His palace is an earthly palace and it is situated in the dump. His kingdom extends to the inner suburbs and overflowing skips everywhere.
- His angels are reversing trucks.
- He is a material and temporal God and His gifts are seldom gold and rubies.
- He is the God of broken or three-legged chairs. He is the God of the discarded, the rejected and the useless.
- Within the cult of the Street God there are tenets of the faith that must be obeyed.
- You must never ask the Street God for specific favours; cardboard boxes are His forte.
- Everything beneath His gaze has equal worth. This is to cover the fact He does not have a discerning eye.
- Never rely on the God of the Street for a birthday, wedding or engagement present.
- Never pretend the Street God has smiled on you when you are stealing.
- If you follow these simple rules you will enter His kingdom.
- Open your eyes to His kindness and you will never fully close them again.

There was a time when I would converse with the God of the Street constantly. His bounty was plain to see, exploding out of skips, at the back of the department store, forgotten at the end of a lane. If you failed to take an item He offered there would always be another to tempt you – a cracked Thermos, an old pair of loafers, a ripped vinyl jacket. His generosity knew no bounds and He was exceedingly good.

I first met the Street God at the tip amid burst green garbage bags oozing pustulant gunk and lockjaw-inducing razor-sharp sheet metal. He was there in mountains of waste rising from valleys of debris laced with rivers of effluent – slag-heap cathedrals to consumer society, glittering in the afternoon sun, with all the promise of capitalism. Here an enamel pendant, a malfunctioning radio or a mayonnaise-stained magazine was a gift from God.

Then someone somewhere, in the safety of an office, decided it was too dangerous. They closed the tips. Yet for every unfortunate who tore their foot apart on a rusty tin there were thousands who would risk life and limb to discover a useless phone or a crushed circuit. There are organisations that recycle rubbish at tips – a noble idea, but it brings no joy to the hunter–gatherer of crap. There is no sense of wonder in finding a piece of rubbish that someone else has already found, picked out of the scrap, polished and presented.

I was thinking that I had not heard from the Street God for a long time. I thought He and I had fallen out. That was when I had the dream. And the dream brought me to a realisation.

There were two sets of hand prints foraging around a skip. I knew one set was mine and the other set belonged to the Street God. I looked again and there was only one set. I asked Him what had happened. Why He had left me? He smiled and replied, 'That was when I foraged for you. You went to take a leak.'

I woke realising the Street God was still with me. Over the years I had changed, not He. I was no longer a disciple, a mere acolyte; I was a priest. I realised as I descended the stairs with my garbage that I was still doing His will. I peered longingly into my own waste – a stack of faded English magazines, a broken Rotring pen, a bent picture frame and a three-legged chair.

My weekly walk to the wheelie bin is an offertory procession and the damaged, worthless scraps I drag there a tribute to the Street God.

The End of Embarrassment

The terrible thing about life is that it comes to an end. We never know how or at what hour we'll be taken from all this glorious wonder. The only thing that's certain is we will die.

The other day I sliced open the top of my left forefinger with a scalpel. It was pure clumsiness on my part that led to this incident. I was feeling happy and momentarily distracted by the TV and the next thing I knew a torrent of blood was jetting from my finger.[1] This minor injury led me to ponder my eventual demise. It's something we all think about: how will it end? For some, brooding on possible deaths is seen as a negative or depressing pastime. For others it's an enjoyable activity to while away a dull afternoon. I tend to fall into the latter category.

It need not be a solitary activity but can be something the whole family can enjoy. Who has never managed to repulse themselves by thinking of a truly gruesome demise? The imagination is a richly textured environment in which to explore that unimaginable moment. There is inevitably great diversity in the desired way to expire (many are fanciful Learyesque options too chemically complex to investigate here – suffice to say that the final hours involve *2001: A Space Odyssey* and a one-way ticket to Tomorrow Land) but there is general consensus on three points:

1. Fire would be a lousy way to go.
2. Drowning would be okay.
3. No-one wants an embarrassing death.

An embarrassing death is any death after which, if you had lived, you'd have said, 'What a stupid thing to do.' *He was checking out a gas leak and he didn't have a torch so he lit a match. He attempted to remove his own appendix with a grapefruit spoon. He sought to breastfeed an orphaned piranha. He had a heart attack with his trousers round his ankles while he was linked up to some filth on the Net.* They're the stories we come across every other day. That embarrassing death that makes the afternoon papers and has people chortling on their way home from work. The sort of death that brings joy to strangers. The sort of death that makes an amusing short film. The sort of death that is preceded by the exclamation: 'Oops!' The sort of death that becomes the after-dinner conversation in inner-city apartments with groups of bloated, coiffured dandies discussing the intimate details of your final gasp. It's bad enough to have your name bandied about while you're living, but imagine the shame once you've gone. Of course, it's something you don't have to live with, but the idea alone is enough to cause you eternal pain in the afterlife.

Almost any death could lead down that avenue to shame. An old gent slips on a banana peel in the shower. Suddenly there are all these questions left unanswered that must be answered in his absence. What was a banana peel doing in the shower? What happened to the rest of the banana? What was the old man doing in a shower miles from his own home?

I have always believed the embarrassing end lies in wait for me because whenever I am ludicrously happy I tend to become life-threateningly clumsy. I have witnessed this type of pathology in many other people, and I'm grateful it's not mine alone (though I must confess that on occasion the 'ludicrous happiness' is a by-product of alcohol, which may affect my motor coordination). Moments of unbridled joy are often accompanied by the proximity of eternal rest. It may have something to do with the feeling of invulnerability we experience when we're truly happy. But happiness is deceptive. It's no defence against a car careening out of the night. And there is no way mirth can protect you from falling crates. And if you have an uncontrollable giggling fit as you're pursued across the Kalahari by ferocious beasts, you'll be torn apart. This may be the reason we're not as funny any more. Evolution has seen to it that only the sensible survive. Happiness momentarily distracts us from the difficult task of living, the difficult task of self-preservation. This is why wild animals are wary of giggling, and you rarely, if ever, see them laugh. Humanity, on the other hand, has built entire cities so we can cack it in safety. When we laugh, we let ourselves go, and in that uniquely human moment we become most vulnerable.

---

1   Every time I have to type the letter r, t, f, or g I feel a moderate amount of pain. When I am forced to bend my slowly healing finger back to reach the c or the v key I am in serious danger of opening the wound afresh. For this is reason there may be a deficiency of words using those letters within this article.

New Dimensions in Space

Corridors are haunting me. They fill my dreams, and in my waking hours I find they enclose me. I am trapped and tortured by the mere thought of them. I see them everywhere as part of everything. I have tried to avoid them but it is to no avail. Once I leave the safety of the room, I am in one. There is another leading to the front door. There is no other way out of the house, so I am forced to use one to leave my own home. Then I find myself in another and another. The places I work are riddled with them. Look around: you could be in one right now. You take them for granted, become oblivious to them, until you realise they are everywhere.

I am not limiting my notion of the corridor to a carpeted stretch of floor from the front door to the kids' bedrooms, a useless antechamber clustered with trinkets, books and framed photos of the family. I see the corridor as any space that serves to separate or 'unite' two distinct areas. Corridors are the spaces between spaces, the segments between rooms. They are meant to link spaces, but to me they create division. In this day and age we have an overreliance on them. They turn our houses into rabbit warrens, our buildings into Swiss cheese, our lives into misery. Picture, if you will, your most potent memory of a corridor. Does it bring any sense of happiness to you? All my recollections are negative. I see a transient world where grief or joy is delivered at the opening of a door. The hospital corridor? The corridor outside the principal's office? The corridor of a prospective employer? The endless, weaving corridors of bureaucracy. I have begun to loathe and fear them. They are an antispace space, a form of architectural purgatory, a linear maze.

There are two popular theories as to their origin. One claims they are descendants of the aqueduct and other forms of Roman plumbing. The lead-lined tubes that carried the ablutions of the empire were enlarged to carry people, the purpose being very similar.

The other is that they became a fundamental part of European architecture during the reign of Victoria and symbolise the worst excesses of puritanism. Their function was to shield, to disguise and to hide. We speak of the 'corridors of power' because we know this is where true power lies, skulking around a corner outside the honesty of the room. They were put in place so delicate conversations could not be overheard, so parents could conceal their passions, so governments could plan and conspire. They were designed to throw up a veil of secrecy and separate age from youth, men from women, knowledge from innocence.

Where a fine room will make a statement, a corridor will always pose a question. If I venture this way, what will become of me? What is at the end of this passage? Even as I write there is one corridor stretching off to my left and another off to my right. When I finish this where am I to go? I am stuck in the middle, a rat at a T-junction.

Of late I have started to wonder about their real purpose. Insidiously they have begun to infiltrate the arts. They have been in paintings and in poems and referenced in songs. Corridors are where most of the action takes place in thriller, horror and adventure films. They are a means of escape from which there is no escape. They have even appeared in mature, dramatic pieces. Bergman was prone to a corridor now and then. They also inhabit the four elements. We have corridors of fire, air, earth and water. (And why is it called the 'green room' when it is clearly a corridor of water? Because the 'green room' sounds like the place to be, while the 'green corridor' sounds like a sewerage outlet.) They lie in wait at cinemas, cathedrals and casinos. Every time you switch on the television you can see them lurking in the background. In most computer games you battle in endless mutating artificial corridors. Lifts are merely cramped vertical corridors that dump you at long horizontal ones. They also come disguised as modes of transport (corridors with wheels) – trains, buses and trams. And what is an aeroplane, if not a corridor with wings?

When we are born we are forced out a corridor of flesh into the harsh glare of life. Is it any wonder that as we depart this world there is another corridor, a corridor of light? That leads us where? No-one who has come back to us has made it all the way along this final corridor. None of them can tell us what's there or where it takes us. The tales of the journey are vague too, often confused, and yet they all agree on one point: a long corridor with a bright light at the end. Is it a passageway to heaven or an afterimage burnt onto the optic nerve as our brains give out? Probably just an infinite corridor. One last eternal joke at our expense.

I look to the right. I look to the left. I can see a world free of the tyranny of the corridor. A world of architectural honesty where rooms come face to face with rooms, open-planned for open minds. Today we have left the corridor of ignorance and opened the doors of perception. Now we know, where do we go to from here?

The Daily Grind

It's Sunday. Let's assume there's a God. Let's also accept that in seven days he created the world. I've been wondering if over the several millions of days since He has given his creation a second thought. Has He cast an almighty eye over us, rubbed His godly chin and thought, 'That colour's not right. I don't like the shape of that tree. I don't know why I put the spots on the leopard.'? Anyone in their right mind would ponder whether He rushed some things to get them done in time. Do all those fault lines need grouting, repairs for wear and tear, to maintain the property?

Does anyone else find the whole night and day thing a bit tedious? We have a period of twenty-four hours divided into two parts by the absence or presence of the sun and moon. Nothing to look forward to but the same dreary old sun up sun down, day in day out, for as long as we live – that brilliantly burning clump of celestial gases as regular as clockwork popping up to greet us every morning. Do you find it a trifle old- fashioned that we're controlled by a couple of lumps in the sky? It'd be spectacular to get up one morning and for the damn thing to surprise us: rise in the west, set in the north, make a U-turn at midday, head back out to sea. It baffles me why the sun, or the creator of the sun, isn't that creative.

And I'm tired of that boring yella moon moving through its phases again and again, suspended overhead like a jaundiced toenail flung into the firmament.

And then there's the seasons. Has anyone else noticed they follow a pattern? Blindly chasing each other without variation: summer, autumn, winter, spring. There are some who speculate the weather is changing. I don't believe it's changing enough. What about another season? Four seems restrictive. Where was the vision behind four seasons? If there were more of them we wouldn't be limited to just football and cricket.

And the sky. Okay so He's had a bit of fun with the random abstract cloud idea, and the way it gives the impression of constant movement. I like the clever way the weather ties in to play off against the blue with a dark or light grey capturing a feeling of mood. But has anyone else looked up and longed for a different colour? Blue's pretty enough, and preferable on a daily basis to something like puce, but a change is as good as a holiday. Anyone who's been to a paint shop lately will tell you there's a lot of very attractive colours out there. I'm not suggest-ing we go with it as a permanent tone, but for one day in five – terracotta with a nice marble effect?

Once the sky is happening, you could do something more with the clouds. Get away from the depressing grey motif and really bring them out of themselves. Radiant magenta or metallic cumulus drifting through strands of tangy orange goat's hair or salmon-tinted nimbus. It'll spin out some of the hippie-trippy acid-casualty flower-power children but that's the price you pay.

The 24-hour-day concept I find limiting. It's functional, and the whole calendar thing was a great idea, but it's gotten to the stage where we live our lives by it. The problem is the hours in the day – there are never enough of them. I suggest we make the hours shorter, cram a few more in, make the days longer. Let's lose the leap year and watch our ordered universe slide into absolute chaos.

And let's have a fresh batch of animals, simply reworking the old themes by putting them together in a different way. The ones we've got are cute enough, but we've seen them for countless centuries and it's time for something new. Freaky unnatural cross-fertilisation would be a good start, with more creatures along the lines of the platypus. An animal that's a hybrid, a hotchpotch: the bubble and squeak of the animal kingdom. Let's get insects and make them colossal and shrink tigers, lions and bears to the size of bugs. I feel unless we get some variation soon we'll have to start making them ourselves. Scientists all over this mess of an earth are itching at the test tube to give birth to their own monsters.

If there is some type of omnipotent patriarch that assembled and oversees our world, then He's left us on the evolutionary spin cycle – set and forget. He's popped out before we began documenting history and He hasn't returned to kick us on to the next level. We're stuck with the scenery going around and around with monotonous regularity. I promise you this: you'll wake up tomorrow (unless of course you don't) and nothing will have changed.

CONCERNING BEASTIES

The Disposition of
Cockroaches

I am at war. I am at war with an adversary who does not recognise the suffering of war or the art of war. An adversary whose resources are limitless and who is more numerous than the stars in the heavens. The cockroach.

To battle the cockroach I have had to think as it does. Our needs are remarkably similar – eat, eat, reproduce, eat. I have put myself in its shell. Each day the differences are becoming less distinct – the boundaries are beginning to blur. I do not exist in a Kafkaesque delusion. I do not imagine I'm a roach. There is still one major difference between the roach and myself: it does not pay rent.

Cockroaches inhabit the same space, they eat the same food, they frolic in the same bed. Under my roof they have the same rights as me. It is a struggle for life and only the strongest will survive. I have bombed, baited, laid traps, mixed obscene concoctions developed on the isle of Haiti, I have danced naked in the moonlight, prayed to pagan gods and killed with my bare thumb. Still the hideous hordes continue to pour from every nook and cranny. It is a bitter battle, and on both sides, the casualties are high.

My allies have fled leaving me alone to face my enemies. The spiders have been scared out of the bathroom, the bedbugs bullied from the pungent cotton wadding of the futon. Cockroaches are the Mafia of the insect world. They have a network. They have an organisation. They have a deal. At night I feel them joining me between the sheets. They feast on my waste – the morsels that flake from my scalp are as tasty as truffles. I am a gourmet's delight for a cockroach, a walking smorgasbord of living treats. An eat-in take-away.

I try to live in harmony with nature, but I live in hatred of cockroaches. Do not mistake me: I do not fear them. The emotion that I feel is deeper and darker than that. It is an awareness of the truth.

My transformation began when they sabotaged my *reward*. That was when the battle became the war. The reward – a bowl of a well-known breakfast cereal – dates back to my childhood and affords me some small comfort when I am feeling depressed. On this night it had quite the opposite effect. Pouring out the golden flakes of corn I noticed a hard, dark husk loitering near the base of the bowl. My eyes being weak and my responses slow, I thought it was nothing more than a 'golden flake' that had been overcooked – a black sheep in a field of corn, a hunk of charcoal, a little bit of cereal gristle. I poured the milk. The gristle moved. It twitched. Its tiny, ugly antennae unfurled. A polished exoskeleton scuttled over my golden flakes. Filled with disgust and revulsion, I picked the offending creature out of the infested mire and crushed it. My long-awaited reward was ruined by the minuscule monster. I was so disgusted I threw the bowl, and all its contents, into the sink. But this incident alone failed to push me over the brink. It was the surprise attack moments later that caused me to snap. I went to change the fax paper. I lifted the hood on the machine and recoiled in horror as five roaches fled the light. This new turn in their campaign shocked me. I had staked out most of the areas that contained food and scrapings of skin, but I never thought that they would attempt to infiltrate the machines. If they are in the fax, is it reasonable to assume they are also in the computer? It may explain why the damn thing continues to betray me.

All methods devised to eradicate them have failed. I have made intricate notes concerning the effectiveness of the various agents of roach death. I am Vlad the Impaler, Genghis Khan, Pol Pot. I am numbered amongst those who enjoy the fever pitch of battle and display their victims as trophies. I have ritualised the deaths of my loathsome adversaries. I wear their shattered carcasses as a necklace. I rejoice. Their severed heads on match-sticks ring the pantry. In *Spartacus* a broken army is crucified to show the resolve of the emperor and what happens to those who oppose his rule. I have crucified the roaches on Paddle-Pop sticks evenly spaced on the main road to the fridge. This is what happens to all who defy the might of Rome.

You may think that all this has brought me some measure of comfort. It has not. The one small joy in death I find is contained within the Cockroach Hotel. What a marvellous device. TV has lost all interest for me. I sit in an armchair and gaze at my captives as they writhe in agony attempting to escape their fate. As they twist out of their skins, snap their limbs, I watch. I have no desire to channel-surf, I have all I need. It's all there on that sticky toxic piece of cardboard – life, death, the eternal struggle. A snuff film in a box.

I have, you may argue, lost my humanity in this struggle. In this war, surrounded by constant death, I have found a clarity to life I have never known before. I have seen the truth and am not afraid to speak it. We all know when we destroy our planet cockroaches will rule the earth. Why do we attempt to delude ourselves: they rule it now.

Concerning the Ibis:
a Dog of a Bird

White feathers brown-grey from the muck and grime of the city. A tiny blackened head foraging for scraps. Its elegant beak pinpointing morsels that shorter-beaked birds cannot reach. It is a superior animal in every respect and it is rewarded for this evolutionary gift with a half-eaten egg-and-bacon sandwich still wrapped in plastic.

Several readers know of my loathing for the cockroach; few are aware of my deep and uncontrollable hatred of the ibis. It is a hatred fuelled by sadness. How could this bird have fallen so far?

The ibis, the treasured bird of ancient Egypt, who possessed a special relationship with the gods. The ibis who inspired the poets Ovid and Callimachus. The ibis, Coleridge's second choice for the albatross, and friend of the phoenix.[1] This once magical bird has fallen further and harder than any other. Maybe it happened when the ibis swapped the banks of the Nile for the sewerage outlets of Bondi. Perhaps when it left the Tigris and Euphrates, the home of civilisation, and settled for the corner of Victoria and Darlinghurst streets, the home of the cappuccino.

One thing is true: the proud bird that left the drifting sands of the mystic East is not the same one that arrived penniless in the antipodes. The ibis has become a vagrant, a hobo, a bum. The only difference is the ibis doesn't have a shopping cart to push around. If you get close enough to one to smell its breath it even reeks of turps. Somehow the ibis became the Robert Downey Jr of the heron family – a gifted creature with an assured future who now stalks the back streets covered in crap, a shadow of its former self, desperately in need of rehab (Robert, not the ibis).

My eyes first alighted on the bird in a book on Tutankhamen. I was trying to complete a school assignment on interbreeding, false gods, water on the brain and pyramids, when there stood the ibis. A divine creature with a long, swan-like neck and stark white feathers. Its noble profile carved into stone by long-dead artisans. A bird with a living body and a tiny mummified head. The more I looked the more the ibis stared back at me from the pages of history. Its sacred image shaped with lapis lazuli, pressed into metal, etched into the walls of Cheops. Those papyrus readers loved that bird. In this old world the ibis knew Osiris and Horus, the gods of ancient Egypt, and roamed free in the gardens of Ramses and Cleopatra. You can tell a lot about a bird by the company it keeps.

These days the ibis is most often seen in the company of pigeons (the rats of the air) and seagulls (the pigeons of the sea). I have no idea what goes on in the mind of the ibis: it may think the other birds look up to it. It's like the big dumb kid at school who hits puberty first, the kid you send in to get fags and booze. The truth is, the only reason those mongrels hang around is to feed on the scraps the ibis drops. These scavengers are using the ibis, and the dwarf stork is too stupid to figure it out. You couldn't fit much of a brain in that cranium and the brain is the one place where size is important. So there it stands, a moronic feathered Fagin surrounded by an assortment of winged rats and seabirds. And thereby hangs a tale . . .

A tiger, a fox and an ibis met one night in the jungle. The tiger said, 'I have these stripes to conceal me in the forest.' The fox said, 'I have these eyes to help me see at night.' The ibis said, 'I have this really long beak to get to all that good stuff at the bottom of the bin.' What a gift? What immortal hand or eye framed that one? Here's a long bill used for probing mud for soft molluscs or for hunting through garbage to find a mouldy falafel fused together with cigarette butts and lemonade. And here are some long legs to help you wade through water or to give you a height advantage when you're raiding the bins.

And so ends a moral story: the ibis is the ugly duckling who grew up to discover it was just a duck, and an ugly duck at that. Where the phoenix rose from the ashes, the ibis rolls around in them, which serves to remind us of the price you pay when you fall from the heavens.

---

1. This is a gross liberty with the truth. What other bird would have the majesty, grace and size to take the place of the albatross? The ibis slung around the neck of a demented mariner would just look like a heavy seventies pendant.

Animals in Advertising

• Part 1

'A dog is man's best friend.' In the earliest transaction between humanity and an animal, dogs agreed to be loyal, subservient companions in exchange for warmth, shelter and food. Part of this agreement meant they would be called upon to perform unpleasant tasks. The most unpleasant and degrading of these would be to appear in commercials.[1]

The world of advertising has entered a new phase with an alarming increase in the number of animal-oriented ads. There have always been the Shirley Temple quadrupeds: 'trained' animals bred to perform. Dogs and cats with shiny coats, good teeth and a carefree attitude to life. The kind of animals that, if they were human, would be in Coca-Cola ads. At least these creatures advertise products that have some impact on their lives, by doing things like chowing down on cow liver or begging to be wormed. But these days all kinds of exotic mammals are working their arses off selling everything from cars to chocolate bars. We have polar bears swigging rum and acting like 'Westies', paragliding three-toed sloths and camels who get off on funk and afros. As our groovy dromedaries head into the sunset it seems every creature has got a licence. What are we being told? That the car is so easy to master even a dumb animal like *you* could do it? Or is this because once behind the wheel we all become animals? In these times of high unemployment it seems our little furry friends are getting all the good jobs – the worker is losing out to four-legged scab labour.

There are many reasons for the popularity of animals: they're cute, cuddly and tell the truth – as opposed to human beings, who are all liars. A panda would never mislead you about the interior comfort of a car, an elephant wouldn't swim for a drink unless it tasted great, and we all accept the fact that polar bears are party animals who dig foxy ladies, bad jazz and getting pissed. I cannot deny the honesty or popularity of animals, but I am concerned about the psychological strain a workload places on a creature of leisure – it could be the straw that breaks its back.

There are safeguards ensuring animals in ads are not physi-cally mistreated, but what of their mental state? They're well fed and pampered now, but there may come a day when they're not needed any more. What happens when the Daewoo dog has finished its hectic schedule of script reading, shooting, perform-ing and mall appearances? What then? What happens if a young pup comes along with more talent? After years of being the top dog in sales will he be happy to be put out to pasture like some retired stud bull? After the limousines, the late nights, the wining and dining, where does the Daewoo dog go? Will Peter Luck scout around dumps in search of our Littlest Hobo for *Where Are They Now?*? Will he appear bloated or corpse-like on *Oprah* as sad and forgotten as a child star? (The Daewoo dog, not Peter

Luck.) Will he end up maggot food and mulch like Skippy, Gentle Ben, Flipper, Charlotte,[2] Rin Tin Tin, Lassie and all the others?

We have all seen the terrible effect that fame and fortune can have on people. What will it do to animals? One need only look at Shirley MacLaine and Marlon Brando. Will our Daewoo dog swell up to the size of a Zeppelin, lose loved ones in a bizarre murder triangle and write best-selling books about self-realisation and reincarnation?[3]

In the fast livin', easy sex, hard drugs and 'dog eat dog' world of advertising, any creature could lose its innocence – despite a willingness to be exploited. Animals will continue to be used in advertising because they're cheaper than child labour, most of them work for peanuts, and they have no conscience. This final factor is most important – it means animals will sell anything, even if they don't believe in it.

This is one issue that has got my goat and where we have to take the bull by the horns, bell the cat, and enter the lion's den. It's not too late, the horse hasn't bolted, and if we're eager beavers we won't end up flogging a dead one. We have to go cold turkey on the whole animals-in-ads thing. Animals are sitting ducks for unscrupulous merchants and if we don't take care of them they'll all be as dead as dodos. So tomorrow, if it ever comes, I'm off to see a man about a dog. We have reduced their numbers and destroyed their habitats, and now we force this final indignity upon them. How long will it be before that bear in the woods is using Sorbent?

---

1. I am not worried about the inhuman use of humans in advertising – they've made a choice. It's the inhuman use of animals that perturbs me.

2. Charlotte was in fact an animated spider and thus not prone to death.
3. A frightening aspect of animals, advertising and reincarnation is that if Tim Shaw were to come back as a panda, there'd be no stopping him.

Animals in Advertising

• Part 2

*[addressing the dilemma of men
and women in animal costumes]*

Poisonous, venomous and ugly creatures that regularly eat children tend not to feature in ads – you may as well hire an actor. Which brings us to the second aspect of animals in ads: some of them are not animals at all. Some of the animals, noticeably the tap-dancing ones or ones with a rudimentary grasp of English, are, in fact, performers. Due to the immense popularity of animals in film and TV there is a hole in the market that must be filled from somewhere. Young, vibrant performers, many from our finest acting colleges, are sucked into this strange world and their dreams of playing *Hamlet* are lost forever. Confined in the back end of a dancing cow or the animatronic skull of a dog, they become cynical and bitter. For these young people 'playing the Dane' has a completely different meaning.

Sadly more and more performers are discovering they're being called upon to play animals. Not just in Berkoff plays, but in shopping malls as Easter bunnies and as tigers to attract traffic. Most of us will never imagine what it's like to be trapped inside tons of rubber, fur and fake hair (unless you're RuPaul). We'll never have our feet turn into talons, will never know what it's like to be stuck inside a polar bear all day, and few of us want to find out.

My awareness of this terrible profession was raised when I met a man called Jack. Jack was up for a part in a new movie called *Godzilla*: a multimillion-dollar epic from the subtle creative team who brought you *Independence Day*. He was short-listed to play the lead, but sadly no-one would ever know it was him, as the anonymity of the animal actor is of paramount importance.[1] No-one would notice him walking down the street and beg for his autograph. There would never be a buzz of murmurs in his local restaurant: 'Look over there, isn't that . . . Godzilla?' He would remain unrecognised, but he could always hold his head high knowing he was a star.

He began his life as a beast working in China, where each day consisted of stomping over papier-mâché buildings and terrorising Tokyo, cutting his teeth on difficult characters such as the boxing kangaroo, a three-legged dog called Kundo and a dancing starfish. He then expanded his repertoire with Mighty Morphin' mechanical half-man, half-plastic monsters.

Jack was true to his art and stayed in character on and off the screen. Stripped of his costume he maintained the mentality of the beast: he refused to talk, preferring to growl; he slept on straw and had poor toilet habits. He lost friends but he found professional acclaim. This was the cost of being the best. Jack excelled with his unique interpretations of these creatures, but as with any actor he longed for the classics. His chance came with a Chinese–European co-production of *Ulysses*. Jack got his wish – he played the Hydra, Cyclops and Cerberus.

After ten years along came Godzilla, the most coveted of all the monster roles. (Godzilla is one of the few creatures perfectly suited to have a man inside it.) There was intense competition for the part. Out of hundreds of applicants they were down to the last three, possibly the finest creature performers in America, if not the world. These were three men who knew how to think like animals, and they weren't even involved in politics.

The moment of truth came when Jack clambered inside the motorised rubber body. In that airless prison of PVC he felt at home and he brought Godzilla to life. With her mighty limbs he tore down buildings, he breathed fire, he crushed cars and menaced children – but at the end of the day he wasn't the one.

It was a painful rejection, an emotional upheaval that forced him out of the business. On contemplation Jack found that staring through the nostrils of monsters gave him a limited vision of the future. With his head removed, the world once again opened before him. Here was a real world that didn't crumple when he touched it, a world where men were men, not Mothra, Zargot or the Toad of Colandot. These days Jack is happier playing a comical father in a popular American sit-com – a father who moves with the grace and poise of a caged animal. He discovered that, in the world of the animal actor, it is we who are the true monsters.

---

1. Donald Arkness played a grizzly bear in a number of fine American TV comedy series from the late forties to the early seventies (*F Troop*, *Leave it to Beaver*, *The Munsters*). He had a great desire to be recognised publicly for his work. This led him to wear the bear costume permanently: to private functions, in coffee shops, at his son's bar mitzvah. When he died, in 1977, he insisted his headstone read, 'Donald, the friendly Grizzly – not dead, just hibernating.'

On the Human Tragedy
of the Bowerbird

'A small figure flits back and forth across the rainforest floor. Between the sagging branches a tiny thief works tirelessly. His keen eye pillages the landscape for morsels that he can use. Discerning and tactful, the wrong colour or shape and the item is immediately discarded. An artisan of the highest order, he returns to his concealed castle and places his newly found twig in. Filled with pride he pauses to survey the majesty before him, an architectural tribute to nature. He possesses the mad desire of Van Gogh, he is the Gaudí of the animal kingdom: the humble and insane bowerbird.'[1]

The bowerbird goes to obscene lengths to attract a mate. It creates lavish structures filled with bright objects, plants 'lawns', builds stages to perform on and occasionally paints interior walls with regurgitated charcoal and vegetable pulp. It longs for an episode of *Our House* or *Burke's Backyard* as humans long for the gift of flight.

There is one reason and one reason only for the strange behaviour of the bowerbird: it has too much time on its hands (and it doesn't even have hands). Bored out of its tiny bird-brain, this evolutionary freak was forced to come up with some inventive way to find a meaningful existence. With surprisingly few predators inhabiting its environment and a plentiful supply of food, the bowerbird has filled up its time in a way that is anything but natural. It may have sat listless with ennui for centuries before the thought of collecting scrap and building a lean-to seemed sensible.

Like the bowerbird we are the most successful creatures in our neck of the woods, having nothing to fear from any other creature. The consequence of this hard-won position at the top of the food chain is that we spend less time fighting for our survival, which leaves us more leisure time. We need something to distract, entertain and occupy ourselves, and like the bowerbird we have found it feathering our nests. We crowd our homes with useless trinkets, discarded toys and mountains of paper, defining ourselves by what we possess. And from these citadels of crap we coo to our prospective partners.

Our major shopping malls are the cluttered landscape where bright, shiny objects lure the 'bowerbird within'. Overcome by our instinct to shop, we spend hours dragging ourselves from cabinet to change room to counter in search of the perfect ornament, the exquisite artefact. It may be a pair of 'moccies', or a plastic shark-tooth pendant, a smart velour windcheater or anything in copper. The human-bower can be found from Harrods to the $2 shop [2] pecking up bargains. What we select indicates our likes and dislikes, our strengths and weaknesses, and like our feathered friend, our little chests puff out with pride when our effort has been noticed. Whose heart has not fluttered when it has glimpsed the object of its desire? Whose heart has not soared when that object has become theirs?

The tragedy is that although we have seen numerous documentaries about this bizarre bird, we have failed to learn the valuable lesson it can teach us. We have failed to see we follow the same imbecilic pattern. We too have a surplus of time. Over the centuries we have weakened ourselves physically and mentally. We have become the knock-kneed, feather-brained, sparrow-chested cousins of the bowerbird. At the moment half this country is complaining about working a measly 35-hour week and the other half is always wanting something for nothing. Everyone wants more money for doing less, and as a net result, all of us are plunged into financial chaos. There is a devastatingly simple solution to this circular trauma: work twice as long for half as much. If we brought back the seventy-hour week (or the ninety-hour week), then people wouldn't have enough energy to complain. At least we'd stop being a nation of whingers. A clear message is being sent to us from the rainforest floor. It's time to wake up and listen to the song of evolution: for the bird of paradise life is hell.

We have always been jealous of the bird, jealous of its ability to fly. From the doomed Icarus to Freudian floating dreams to air travel, we have yearned for the limitless freedom of the sky. The sad truth is that if we were born with wings they'd be the wings of the bowerbird and life would remain essentially the same.[3]

---

1. This extract is taken from Tarquin Regent's *The Secret Life of the Bower* (1952). A literary giant amongst naturalists, he was admired for his passionate studies of the *Ptilonorhynchidae* family. His life was to end in tragedy, however, when he confessed an unnatural and forbidden love for a yellow-breasted bullfinch.

2. I am a great believer in the $2 shop, although with current financial trends, these true Australian institutions could be lost for future generations. How could we possibly explain in the $5 shop the happy days when everything was $3 cheaper?

3. There is no doubt that I have taken liberties with extended poetic licence.

The Web of Life

There it goes again. I know what it is but I don't want to look up, I don't want to be disturbed. It's just loud enough to draw my attention away from the paper, away from what I'm concentrating on. The noise sits on the outer edge of my hearing. Other incidental sounds are louder, sharper, but it possesses one quality they do not: repetition. There it goes again: a flat, inconstant hum followed by a dull, wet thud and a moment of recovery. Then it begins again.

I am determined not to look up, and I know it wants me to look, wants me to stop enjoying the paper and acknowledge its pitiful existence. It's been going for five minutes now and I don't think it's going to end. It has no mind to grasp the annoyance it's causing me. I become more intent on the newspaper, more focused, even though I am not reading anything. My eyes are running over words that are nothing more than squiggles. The angles and forms of language have been lost to me. I'm staring at sheets of unintelligible grey printed paper but my mind is on the fly. I put the paper down and look at the contemptible insect.

I watch the big, fat blowie wander up a pane of glass

aimlessly searching for an opening. It's drawn to the light and the lush garden beyond, the garden with its promise of dead and rotting things. A tube protrudes from the tiny monster's head, moist and sticky, exploring the window. Twitching fibrous legs gain easy purchase on the smooth surface. It swivels, flies up an inch or two, accompanied by the drone, before smashing its useless head against the same pane of glass. Outside grey clouds have swamped the little house where I'm staying.

The blowfly passes from one pane to another, bulbous segmented eyes pounding against the invisible barrier. I witness the uselessness of its actions, the hopelessness of its situation, and can't help but think of myself. (It's not that I can relate every-thing back to me, but in this situation it does seem particularly pertinent.) I have been handed a visual template for existence: the fly. I wonder if its minuscule brain is grappling with this dilemma.

Perhaps the giant will give me a big, damp bowl of sugar.

Fate has forced us to be companions this afternoon while I'm certain all the fly wants is food. It wants to be vomiting mucus onto a rancid hunk of beef, reproducing by laying maggots in some warm open wound. The last thing it wants is to be here with me, one of us trapped by the incomprehensible and the other in a quandary over the futility of existence.

Perhaps the giant will reach over and save me from myself.

I have no desire to play God – to let it live by guiding it to an open window or destroying it with a hefty dose of Baygon. I have no need to lord over the lesser creatures or to impose my will on their miniature worlds. The battle for life is played out billions upon billions of times in these mindless scenarios and this microdrama must find its own resolution. This is one insignificant scene from a universe of pain. Between the intermittent buzz I contemplate our own daily struggle, our highs and lows, our joys and sorrows. I think of the difficulty of life, the choices we make that seem monumental but lead inevitably to the same inescapable fact: existence is meaningless and hopeless. (We are all trapped by invisible barriers that stop us getting to the rotting garden.) I am in a free fall of existential angst spiralling down into darkness. Then I realise the buzzing has stopped and I emerge in a room filled with peace and silence.

During my reverie the world has quietly changed. Beyond the windows the mist has melted back to reveal an achingly beautiful sky of the softest pale blue, and here and there the sun has started to warm the earth. I notice the insect that began the journey with me has also gone. The relentless pounding of its frame has been replaced by birds calling to each other from the eucalyptus trees.

While absorbed in my thoughts that I was oblivious to the fact that the fly had escaped, but I now realise that there is hope for us all. In the most dire situations we must never give up, never give in. There is always a way through, a way to triumph, to persevere against unimaginable odds, maintain the lust to live and survive. I feel the fly had been sent to me with this exquisite and wondrous message. At least that is what I feel in the scant seconds before I see the fly again. There is no mistaking that this is my fly. In the bottom corner of another pane of glass the ugly black-green body is covered with sticky white strands of web. Its every movement manages to wrap it more tightly in the arachnid's trap. The drone has become a pale imitation of itself: it sounds pathetic, weaker, accepting. Beneath the struggling body six hollow fly carcasses are a testament to the spider's skill and hunger. For some reason I think of Vincent Price, Jeff Goldblum and myself. Such is life.

Help me, please, help me.

In Praise of Society

The Olympics

We are facing a crisis of confidence. Our national identity and the amorphous Australian psyche is under threat. In the next few years the character of this country may be radically redefined or changed forever.

We've been content to be the 'forgotten continent', the lost island allowing a trickle of fortunate foreigners to savour the splendour of the lucky country. We've only ever made the international gossip columns with stories of dingoes, babies and tennis heroes. Our isolation allowed us to develop an independent spirit, a larrikin nature, but most importantly, it allowed us to be overlooked.

Yet overnight Australia has become the world's oyster. Sydney is the place to be at the end of the century (according to Oprah), and in America they've finally realised we're nowhere near Germany. This sudden awareness began when Sydney was selected as the site for the 2000 Olympic Games. It may well become the darkest day in Australia's history.

For most of us the actual staging of the games is secondary to that momentous moment when an envelope was opened, a syllable was added, and the games were ours. As a nation we felt the ticker tape break on our collective chest. We were winners and we were guilty of every vulgar emotion that accompanies victory – self-righteousness, pride and, in some circles, arrogance. The little Aussie battler had won a major international competition and was instantly transformed into the little Aussie prick.

The years rolled on and the sweet taste of victory corroded to acidic bile. Thus, in these days of Olympic ennui, the advertising world has been called upon to remind us of the wonder of winning. They're attempting to drum up in our deflated hearts a patriotic fervour, to send us over the top for Howard and country, with stirring images and an uplifting song. In the song, a piece of anthemic codswallop, there's an irksome reference that could leave you unsettled in your Jason recliner. As the melody reaches a crescendo, we are referred to as 'the chosen people'. Admittedly poetic licence was taken with this line. It's a romantic notion to be considered the chosen people, to prevail against the odds, and in a real sense we were 'chosen' over Beijing and Manchester. However if we're being totally honest it wasn't really a choice of Sophiesque proportions.[1] And besides, if we go around stomping on the ground, singing out loud that we're the chosen people, it may cause more problems than it's worth. There are several minority groups, nations and organisations who would claim they are the true chosen people. These chosen people have God on their side (whichever God it is) while we, at best, have the Olympic committee.

If we are to retain our national character we must act now. We have two options open to us. The first is to purposely stuff up the games. We could put razor blades on the vaulting horse, grease up the Greco-Roman wrestlers and fill the dive pool with foam. Or we could just let people complain about the contaminated water[2] and the lack of toilet facilities for vegetarians.

The second option is the more compelling – give the games back. How magnanimous and inspirational it would be if we returned that slightly soiled Olympic flag; if, in an act of unparalleled generosity, we offered the 2000 games to our rivals. Socially speaking, China is coming along in leaps and bounds, and with global warming Manchester is getting a bit of sun. Come 2000 do we really want millions of pesky foreigners taking guided tours through our until-recently-untouched wilderness? Do we want our wonderful secret of sun and surf, deserts and snow-covered peaks to be beamed to billions of homes throughout the world? It will only create an atmosphere of international jealousy, with the old, new, first, second and third worlds all coveting our patch of turf.

To call ourselves 'the chosen people' is symptomatic of the way our perception of self is being altered. We are moving from the uncultured antihero slob to the pesto-and-rocket-loving aesthete, from the underdog to Der Über-Hund. If truth be known most Australians only wanted to win the games to beat Ol' Blighty and that other evil empire; putting them on is too much of a bother. If the games are about anything it's the slightly flawed concept that we all get together in friendship to compete against each other. In 1956 the world allowed us to slip back into obscurity; it's doubtful we will be so fortunate this time around. It may be time for the chosen people to make a choice.

---

1. Manchester: a savagely depressed city where it constantly rains. The track and field would have become the track and mud, and how could

any records have been broken running knee deep in waste? External activities would have been limited to being beaten up at the shopping mall. Beijing: the only international record China held at the time was for human rights abuses, and it's doubtful synchronised tank movement could have become an Olympic event.

2. In the dwindling hours of the 20th century Australia's wannabe capital suffered a crisis. It was reported that there were unacceptably high levels of bacteria in the tap water. This proclamation drove some people to panic and resulted in the widespread stockpiling of bottled water.

    Politicians caught in the blaze of media scrutiny were unprepared for the wave of hysteria that was about to crash into them. Committees were formed, subcommittees were spawned and an industry arose overnight to battle the microscopic menace. There were accusations and counter-accusations and lists of questionable statistics that only served to further muddy the water. Since that crisis time has passed and the citizens of Sydney can now drink directly from the tap (which is their God-given right). And I may be mistaken, but in the end it was generally agreed that the initial claim was a mite wide of the mark, that the levels of crap in the water were fine and a little bacteria never hurt anyone.

    For more information about this dilemma please refer to 'The Unseen Dangers of Water' (p. 150) and 'The Survival of the Fittest' (p. 299).

The Ruthless Pursuit of

Happiness

All of us have heard the phrase 'ignorance is bliss', but do we comprehend it?

To understand ignorance we need to look at America. The cornerstone of the American constitution is the 'pursuit of happiness'. However, the Americans don't just pursue happiness, they give it a head-high tackle. They pull happiness to the ground and brand it. How is it they can be so happy? They don't have to try hard, they just don't think about it.[1]

This is the nation that gave us cheese in a can. Eighty-seven per cent of Americans believe that Elvis is alive. Sixty-five per cent believe Jesus was an alien. Fifteen per cent have been sodomised by a ghost and thirty-nine of them, in the Heaven's Gate cult, all wearing Nikes, went to join a spaceship in the tail of a comet.[2] When the Yanks say 'Just Do It' they really mean it. In America an executive decision is choosing between Coke and Pepsi, and the *X-Files* is a documentary.

The truth is out there, and as far as the Americans are concerned it can stay out there. That is why they're so happy.

Hillary Clinton said, 'It takes a village.' I'd say it takes a village idiot! And he became president.

Speaking of Ronald Reagan, he is going through a difficult time at the moment. He is suffering from Alzheimer's disease, and it has reached a stage in which he no longer recalls he was the president of the USA Which isn't that surprising because I seem to have erased that period from my mind as well. This loss of memory does lend some weight to his testimony during the Irangate scandal. Perhaps his failure to recall anything had less to do with perverting the course of justice and more to do with the fact that his brain was turning to mush. He no longer remembers he was the most powerful man in the world. He no longer remembers 'the Gipper'. He no longer remembers what he could not recall when he was called upon to remember. But apart from being permanently confused, he seems to be quite happy.

When were you last truly happy? Peel back the years of misery and you will find a time of unparalleled rapture. It was before you were educated – in preschool. Preschool, before school, when the most intelligent thing you did was 'quiet time'. When you lay there on the heated floor cocooned in a world of silent wonder, beautifully stupid, blissfully ignorant. Preschool, just one year before the terrible realisation in first class that the world was a sham – a shallow pretence built on a flimsy framework of deceit. Your parents were liars, Santa didn't exist, the bionic man was just a dream, and a single world currency would never be achieved in your lifetime.

A little knowledge is a terrible thing. I cannot remember anyone saying 'intelligence is bliss'. The greatest minds of the last few centuries have been stuck in a spiral of misery. You would think if they were so smart they could make themselves happy. Einstein was constantly complaining. His solution to saving energy was wearing the same shirts day in, day out. Here was a man who didn't have a bad-hair day, he had a bad-hair life. Artists, writers, scientists and intellectuals have suffered needlessly for their art. From Nietzsche to Hemingway, from Van Gogh to Sartre, they all went mad, killed themselves or had funny-looking eyes.

Our desperate search for knowledge and self-improvement is holding us back from true happiness. The truth is we think too much.

The Bible says the birds in the field are happy. You ever wondered why the birds in the field are so happy? It's because they're stupid. It's not because the lord God gives them all they need. It's because they don't understand logarithmic progressions, systems of weights and pulleys or modern methods of amputation. Animals are stupid. That's why we call them dumb – 'dumb animals' – and that's why they're happy. Rhinos don't worry about meeting the mortgage repayments on the Serengeti. Dolphins don't think, 'Gee, should have sent the kids to the private school.' Pandas don't have to colour-coordinate the bathroom. They don't fight over whether the bidet should be salmon pink or puce. They don't have to worry that they've reached forty-five, their family has left them, there's no-one to turn to, they have no prospect of a job, the big black lump growing on their flank is a malignant tumour.

In the popular film *Babe* a pig was happily ignorant of the fact he wasn't a sheepdog. He was unaware he was nothing more than leg ham and middle rashers. In *Animal Farm* George Orwell wrote, 'War is peace, freedom is slavery, ignorance is strength.' Was this meant to be sarcastic? Perhaps not, for many a true word is said in jest. Ignorance is strength and that little pig proved it. So what if they roll around in their own shit – it's a small price to pay for happiness.

The truth is out there. Let's keep it out there. The way to a happier life is through ignorance – ask anyone; just ask them slowly.

---

1. I do not condone the practice of generalisation, but it is a simple solution to complex issues.

2. These statistics are falsified, but this should not affect their credibility.

Deconstructing Construction

Sunday morning and my recently attained sleep is shattered by the fire alarm in a nearby block of flats. An armada of screaming fire engines arrives but it's all sound and fury and, significantly, no fire. The apologies and giggles of embarrassment are almost enough to lull me back to sleep around 9 a.m. Thankfully a tone deaf electrician, singing a medley of seventies disco classics, arrives around 10 a.m. to fix the faulty alarm. I'm not against free expression, I just believe that it should be practised in the privacy of one's own home (and practised quietly).

In their nomadic wanderings the noise-makers have scoured most of our country, their blisteringly harsh unexpected sounds infiltrating, penetrating, permeating every part of our lives. They've forced their way into our quiet time, destroyed our peace of mind and now seek to infest our brains.

Over the Christmas break I had the opportunity to stay in various cities across this wide land and I experienced the jarring noises of each: a Perth hotel was remodelled as I tried to sleep, in Melbourne the house next door was demolished, in Sydney roads were reshaped, in Brisbane a car alarm sounded for three days. (Conversely, in Canberra I begged for a little sound yet it maintained its eerie silence.)

The only joy my ears received over this break was the comparative quiet of air travel. If you ignore the turbo-charged lawnmower moaning of the jet engines, the teething babes and the hysterical claustrophobes then it's almost restful. The best aspect of flying is that it's difficult to make repairs while in midair. It's a relatively safe bet there'll be no unexpected maintenance crews hammering away at the aileron at 40 000 feet as you begin the traumatic post-film slumber.

Back on the ground it's a different story. Is there any airport in this country that isn't being rebuilt? As you leave the airport, any road that it isn't being replaced? As you reach the city, any block that isn't undergoing transformation? And when you arrive at the sanctuary of your home there is invariably some prat[1] next door renovating.

It may be the unfortunate side effect of those damnable home improvement programs: 7 a.m. Saturday morning every idiot with a hammer drill wants to use it to create a fashionable painted-pine toy box, or pine tool rack, or much-needed pine toothbrush holder. Out come the rusted circular saws and sanders, their atonal squealing melding with the annoying currawongs to compose a distorted symphony to the dawn. Then there's the restless traffic, the unoiled buses, the non-muffled motorbikes, the untrained busking jazz band, the malfunctioning washing machine, the hum of the fluoros – the list is endless.

It's considered beneficial for the economy that the wheels of industry are turning, but do they have to turn so loudly? The reworking of the world has become so frenetic round my neck of the woods that from one day to the next I cannot recognise the place where I live. We must start to catalogue what was, because it won't be there for long. A building is torn down, another one thrown up. There's always a barrier, or a new fence, or some hideous council-approved sculpture blocking the door. The only thing these changes to our environment have in common is that they make noise, and lots of it.

The cumulative effect of this is frightening: high-tension wires look more relaxed than most of us. We live in a state of extreme agitation. What we need is the soothing sound of an authority figure screaming, 'Shut up, all of you, just shut up!' But who would hear them above the clamour.

We have almost forgotten what silence sounds like (knock on wood). We exist in a world where construction, road works, renovation, fire alarms and burst water pipes are an ever-present threat. We're the victims of a continuous aural assault of random noise. And I've come to the conclusion, as demented as it may sound, that these sounds are intentional.

I've become so obsessed by this paranoid thought that the workmen and workwomen are no longer just working outside – they've managed to infiltrate my head. At night I can hear jackhammers chewing through the soft grey concrete of my left hemisphere, widening the grand longitudinal canal. Urgent and much-needed repairs are being made to my cerebellum. Cracked water mains have flooded the marshlands of my memory and it is drowning. Everything is pushing in on me. Perhaps it is merely cyclical – these things are often cyclical. I will wait patiently for the gentle return of silence.

Sunday morning and the electrician has failed in his attempt to fix the faulty alarm . . .[2]

1. I used the word 'prat' here because this is a family publication and I was not permitted to use the more abrasive, yet technically correct, term '****'.

2. This article was later used by the Department of Education. I have recorded my reaction to its inclusion as a learning exercise in the piece 'The Burden of the Old School Tie' (p. 267).

The Value of the Uniform

We live in a world dominated by difference. In this world of disparate forces, of violence and calamity, it is not music that will bring us together – it's a piece of cloth. It's the uniform, that other universal language, understood by all peoples. To define, delineate and defend there is nothing more unifying than a uniform. Whether it's worn into battle or the classroom it makes a statement, it declares your rank, denotes your occupation or your position in an organisation – it announces your presence. Now the uniform is under attack. It is under attack from the very people who wear it. It is an attack from within.[1]

Over the last three decades the myth of the individual has been accepted across the globe. This has led those engaged in menial labour or servitude to question authority. They have demanded equal pay, to be protected in the workplace, to be treated with respect, to wear what they want to wear. This final indignity is a direct attack on the uniform and began in the schools in the midsixties. School children with weak liberal-minded dope-taking parents were allowed to express their individuality by wearing whatever their little hearts desired. Are we surprised, thirty years on, that three-quarters of the population is illiterate? Illiterate and happily wearing thongs to school. It doesn't end there. In the armed forces, police and clergy, there are go-getter fashion activists who are stripping the uniform of its power.

I will give you one example as a template to understand the danger this poses to society: the uniformed, mounted police officer vs the casual-look cop on a bike.

When the conflict of ideals turns sour and the battle of words becomes a real battle, the uniform has invariably been in the front line. Watching a precision team of riot police twirling batons and decimating sparrow-limbed academics is a marvellous thing. A well-dressed police person astride a mighty heaving stallion, flecks of spittle dried on its flanks and ready to charge, is a powerful and frightening image. Often just the sight of mounted police is enough to discourage would-be demonstrators from senseless acts of demonstration. The uniform and the horse moving with balletic splendour, ranks shattering, the students falling, skulls popping under hoof.

Ask yourself this question: when the hour of truth comes will the police force be up to it mounted on bikes, wearing shorts with ankle-high white socks? I think not. Figure-hugging shorts have never really made it as the attire of oppression. It may have something to do with the musculature of the kneecap appearing humorous in most people. And it's doubtful whether a bike could instil the same sense of fear in a group of blood-crazed demonstrators. Even the classic 1972 'chopper' with streamers on the handlebars and a double-length banana seat wouldn't be up to it. The bike helmet, while essential for protection of the scone, is often not a good look over the plump, red, wheezing face of an unfit constable. Then there is the sad indignity of the bike when faced with a steep incline. I have witnessed a cop, sweat pouring from his brow, flecks of spittle drying on *his* flanks, overcome with exhaustion, pushing the useless hunk of metal to the top of the rise. It says a lot about our society when, these days, all a villain has to do is find a hill and the chase is over.

Still I have nothing but praise for the police in this attempt to blend in with the community. But how long will it be until they're on skateboards and rollerblades in black Lycra thongs and tank tops tagging trains? Or before soldiers want to go into battle with platinum wigs, printed floral gabardine slacks, boob tubes, sandals and facial hair? Does it matter if they're all wearing it? Yes, it does.

It's important as we attempt to integrate various institutions into society that we do not become generic, that our figures of authority do not become figures of fun. What will happen to the rich, textured fabric of society if business people stop power-dressing or if the clergy all adopt casual gear? We are defined by what we wear: clothes maketh the man and the woman and the celibate. Why change the habits of a lifetime? Birds and bees do it – why are we any different? And this pathetic attempt at justification by saying uniforms are oppressive is totally transparent. Of course they're oppressive: that's what they're meant to be. If we continue in this farcical attempt to be like 'the people' we will achieve it and no-one will know who anyone is.

Society needs structure. To enforce structure you need recognisable forces. Bear in mind that without a wimple there never would have been a Flying Nun. If this world does come apart at the seams because we've lost respect for the uniform, then sadly, we'll all just have to wear it.

---

1. This all sounds slightly totalitarian, but hell, it's telling it like it is.

Temptation and Fulfilment

I can understand how in attracting customers a restaurant may wish to make a dish seem more alluring. One dessert that has hooks in its name is *Death by Chocolate*. I have witnessed friends salivating with the mere thought of the ultimate demise. I wonder whether *Death by jellied eel in sow's stomach* has as much appeal.

In the wee small hours, when naming a cocktail, the most ridiculous and obscene thing may appear best. We have all giggled with childish delight when a drunken office worker demands from a bored bartender, '. . . three *Orgasms*, for me and me mates'. But why call a cocktail an *Orgasm*? It doesn't look, taste, or feel like an orgasm,[1] although very occasionally (and I stress very occasionally) it may lead to one.

Giving inventive, embarrassing names to drinks, desserts or perfumes makes sense, especially if you've had a drink. What doesn't make sense, to me, is calling meat and three veg *Longing*. We live in a world where language and meaning are heading in different directions. A world where *Death by Chocolate* is preferable to death before dishonour. Where *Opium* can be purchased over a perfume counter. Where a child thinks an *Act of God* is a choc-coated double-banana treat in an ocean of peppermint cream.

Last week I found myself confronted by this phenomenon several times.

Looking down a menu to find an appropriate dish I was confused. This was not because I was in a Danish restaurant and could not recall too many great Danish recipes. (This is in no way an attempt to insult the Danes and I am sure that were I to think about it the Danes would have as many wonderful recipes as any other nationality.) My dilemma was caused by the fact that every meal had a weird title. Not weird because the names were Danish but weird because they weren't. On the menu were words I was familiar with but had never associated with food. The chicken stew with pepper and caper became *Bewitchment*; braised veal rolls with olives, *Impulse*; the hot and spicy lamb casserole, *Reckless*. There was *Anger*, *Ambition*, *Fantasy* and *Fury* – it'd be like eating the *Gladiators*.[2] That thought alone was enough to turn my stomach before I even considered an entree.

The waiter's pad would have been a surrealist's dream; every time someone ordered, bizarre poems were formed:

2 Longings, 1 medium-rare Enchantress,
1 Temptation, 1 double Eternity holding the mayo,
1 Reckless – not too hot, 3 lo-fat Utopias,
water for the table, screwdriver, rusty nail!

The meals arrived and a general mood of satisfaction prevailed. There was one problem: no-one had accepted the

Temptation. For a minute the waitress circled the table, growing steadily more annoyed.

'*Temptation*? *Temptation* for anyone?'

Nobody moved – most were too busy getting stuck into their own plates of moral and philosophical dilemma.

'Someone ordered it. Who was it?'

'Maybe they've gone?'

Her voice became shrill with tension, and it was clear, despite her outfit, that she was not Danish.

'Who wanted the *Temptation*?'

No-one stirred and the *Temptation* returned from whence it came. If only all forbidden fruits could be sent back so easily to the devil's kitchen.

None of this would have been strange had it not been for what happened next . . .

The following day, as I wandered dazed from lack of food, I found myself before a perfume store. Tendrils of sticky sweet odours lured me into the shop. There were slender bottles of musk, civet and lavender and flasks of essential oils. From floor to ceiling the place was filled with exotic distillations. I ran through a number of perfumes before discovering, with horror, that some of them were last night's meals. There again was *Longing*, *Excitement* and *Passion*.

One perfume in particular held more promise – *Fulfilment*. To my surprise the tester was empty. Obviously this particular fragrance was in great demand. I battled my initial fear, turned to the nearest member of staff, and asked, 'Could you possibly find me a little *Fulfilment*.'

The staff were shocked to learn someone had forgotten to restock that particular scent. No need for concern, there would have to be some *Fulfilment* out the back. I heard them frantically tear apart box after box in search of it. They looked at each other with accusation in their eyes. Somewhere in this jungle of aromas the odour du jour had gone missing. Tension rose as they searched for the scent. A whisper went round the disgruntled customers – 'No *Fulfilment*!'

The woman returned, a little out of breath, a fine sweat beading on her forehead. 'I'm sorry, Sir', she said, 'We can't find *Fulfilment* anywhere!'

I smiled, because in my heart, I sensed she was right.

---

1. In my limited knowledge.
2. A powerful life-affirming TV show with enduring and positive role models (apart from the one who got caught).

The Mythology of the
Rubber Glove

Our hermetically sealed life is under threat. We're being poisoned by our own naivety, by our belief in a myth. Its mere presence can instil confidence or fear. It's worn in virtually every walk of life from the anaesthetist to the zoo-keeper. It's the rubber glove. How can we continue to trust that by seeing a rubber glove on someone else's hand *we* are protected? If a customs official approaches you with grinning teeth, fingers splayed, talc'd gloves at the ready, is it to protect you or them? When a doctor drags out another set of disposable 'medical mittens', are they interested in your health or their own? I tell you this in all honesty: we've been sold a lie. We have to accept the only things the rubber glove protect are the hands of the person who's wearing them.

Probing, prodding and puncturing is one thing, but it's the other end of the problem that interests me: the short-order cook, the kitchen hand, the miscreant wielding a tub of lard. I'm concerned about food preparation.

I once believed in the sanctity of the glove. I believed the myth that by merely covering grubby hands we created a brave clean world. I believed because years ago I experienced an emasculating moment of fear – a fear that forced me into becoming an advocate for the glove. It happened in Canberra. An acquaintance of mine was working his way through university making lunches at a popular sandwich bar. I visited him there once and it was there I witnessed the horror. He was an extra-ordinarily jolly young man. He'd entertain the workers with his infectious good humour as he sliced great wedges of wholesome white bread. He told wonderful stories and lewd jokes, and was so popular that people would queue to have their specific orders made by his hand. The thing they didn't realise was that his hands were in quite bad shape. If they had only looked down. If they had only seen the terror behind the counter. If only they knew, as his hairy knuckles descended into the guacamole, that he had dermatitis.

I witnessed dried slivers of flesh, like bonito fish flakes, curl and fall from his fingers. The blotched redness of his palms. The split dry skin. The matter that oozed up through the fissures and cracks trying to mend the tiny tears that crisscrossed his palms. I could almost smell the pungent aroma of decay drift across the bain-marie. There he was, shedding his snake-like skin into the health salads and strength-restoring sangas of our public servants. Does it make a lot of difference to your well-being if you have white or brown bread with a handful of human crackling? It was nauseating to discover cannibalism, on a minuscule scale, in the corner deli. When I asked why he didn't wear gloves he was offended. Apparently it made his dermatitis worse. He continues to work in Canberra and is still a part of so many public servants' lives and diets.[1]

Over the past week I have changed my mind on the need for

the glove. Three terrifying events have caused me to rethink my position on our sanitary practices. The first of the three occurred at a restaurant when a gloved hand came to grips with an annoying rash around the testicles before tossing a salad. The second was at the 'function of the year'. A cook efficiently stopped her nose from running by stifling the flow of mucus with a polyurethane finger. The same finger she moments later used to wipe away a spillage of gruel from a party-goer's plate. The third was at a pizza parlour where a nonchalant scratch dislodged a large ball of wax that was kneaded into the dough.

These incidents made me realise what we need more than protection is understanding and education. Our hands perform certain functions (itching, scratching, fiddling) and I fear that they perform those functions whether or not they're housed in rubber. Let us look past the gloves and see what the hands have been doing.

I believe I speak for all hygiene-minded Australians when I say: give me an anally retentive 'the germs are out to kill me' cleanliness freak with bare hands rather than an arse-scratching, nose-picking gutter dweller with rubber gloves on. If we're ever to take our rightful place on the world stage it must be with clean hands and a clear sense of personal hygiene. Let us continue to wear rubber gloves, but let us continually remind ourselves why we're wearing them. They're there for the health and safety of those we serve, not to ease our own momentary discomfort or the continual irritations of our diseased limbs.

---

1. Canberrans: I don't wish to instil in you a perpetual fear of your daily bread but the sandwich bar is still operating and Mr Dermatitis is still serving himself as part of a BLT. His name is Alan. I can say no more.[2]

2. Shortly after this article appeared in the paper I received a facsimile from a concerned Canberran working at the Department of Health. I believe it was thought that if the flaky-skinned perpetrator was still around he should be brought to justice (or at least have his diseased limbs sheathed in loving rubber). I was asked to contact the Department of Health as soon as possible. There was an urgency in the fax that disturbed me and it may have troubled me so much that I unconsciously misplaced it. Ever since that day I have been kept awake by the image of an anorexic civil servant condemned to wander Canberra's roundabouts too terrified to eat out.[3]

3. To understand the full horror of being a lost soul in Canberra please read 'The Heart of the Capital' (p. 119).

The New Aesthetic

of Aggression

It was midafternoon on a nondescript day in an ordinary back street of a common-garden-variety suburb when something atypical occurred. Nothing could have prepared me then for what I know now. Nothing will stop the reverberations of horror and uncertainty that continue to plague me. Nothing will allow me to walk the streets without fear of an attack. I have looked into the black heart of the new aesthetic of aggression.

In years gone by the semblance of aggression was easy to recognise: 18-hole Docs, red bigot laces, stretch or stonewash denim, shaved head or a mullet cut, men in groups of three or more often accompanied by a barely restrained, ferociously hungry pit bull. And if indelible proof was needed – the full-face spider-web tattoo in prison-ink blue.

On this day there was only one of those signs: three lads swaggering with intent, dressed deceptively in the height of slacker fashion. If it wasn't for the aura of contained mischie-vousness they could've stepped out of a Mooks catalogue. Beige three-quarter-length cargoes, loose-fitting Ts with pertinent comments about the futility of existence and dark suede Camper boots. They looked like three of the more butch members of Five. If Mary Poppins were alive and a man and living now, she'd look like this.

All that was needed to transform this quiet street was a catalyst. It arrived in the shape of a contented older gent. He stepped onto his verandah, senses dulled by an afternoon nap, vulnerable to attack. The verandah was his pride and joy, clustered with cacti and succulents in terracotta bowls. He rubbed sleep from his tired eyes, tipping a small amount of water on his Green Angel. Then it happened. Before either of us had a chance to react. The leader of the slack, head tilted in a Jimmy Dean post-accident snarl, aimed his pristine teeth at the weary home owner, then in a voice just days from breaking spat, 'Sandstone verandah sux.'

The householder stumbled back, shocked by the seeming stupidity of the insult or mortally wounded by it(?). It was grammatically incorrect and misspelt. I missed a step rubbernecking in awe. The two cohorts of the acerbic villain grinned. They patted their chum on the back, congratulating him on another superior slur. 'Sandstone verandah sux.' Surely a personal attack would have been more effective – something about his failure in life, the stooped back, the sleepy look, the fact that his pyjama bottoms gaped. Why strike out at the verandah? Why not throw a few 'f' words in there, and a couple of emphatic 'c's? The hard consonants of those words are always effective and are guaranteed to shock old, young, women, men, dogs and cats alike. 'Sandstone verandah sux.' The words repeated, looping around each other in a dizzying spiral of confusion and cruelty. And I realised it was clever, too damn clever. This insult would work its magic slowly. It would turn in the old man's heart like a screw.

Most of us have forgotten the fights of years gone by. The broken bones, scabs, cuts, bruises and abrasions have all long since healed. But the words we said would never hurt us still do. The japes and asides, the clever, cruel and carelessly constructed lines, are still with us and always will be.

Under the stinging nettle of the line, my sense of social duty evaporated. I was terrified they'd turn their vitriol on me. (I was poorly dressed for any sour-tongued attack: my mother's hand-knitted poncho had left me wide open.) The lads owned the pavement, the owner retreated inside and I walked on.

How can society protect itself from such garrulous attacks? Will our gardens, homes and floral arrangements be critiqued by *Wallpaper*-reading thugs? What if this is a trend? What if flick knives and guns become passé and ridicule becomes the weapon of choice? Where could you hide? What protection can the police provide from a well-aimed, informed and concise quip? Would we form vigilante groups of smart-mouthed do-gooders to counter this threat? How can you defeat the truth? For in the end they were right. The sandstone verandah did suck. It sucked big time. The off-hand comment enabled me to see the verandah for what it really was. It was sandstone. It was a sandstone veran-dah. I realised, with some sadness, the old codger would be feeding mushrooms before it came back into vogue.

I passed by the house again yesterday. The owner looked dishevelled, older. He sadly shuffled in slippered feet to the edge of the verandah. I could see the loss in his eyes. His love of this verdant shelter with its overhanging pots and healthy plants was shaken and would never fully recover. He stood framed between the pillars in his own green-tinged hell, silently mouthing the words over and over again: 'Sandstone verandah sux.'

On Confronting the
Street Interrogator

Why me? Out of a streetload of potential failures why do they always pounce on me? What am I doing that attracts their attention? Is it something in my manner? Am I the only member of the herd with a limp? Is there blood on my flank? I'm a magnet for anyone with a clipboard and a questionnaire. They'll cross the street to stop me.

Hello Sir, would you like to answer a few questions?

This must be asked of everyone but it seems to be asked of me much more often. It always happens on a busy street corner when I'm trying to get somewhere in a hurry. An earnest stranger, with the conviction of the converted, holding a clipboard, blocks my way.

Just a few questions, it won't take a second.

A multiple-choice minefield to prove, scientifically, that I'm an abject failure. Thirty or so pointed questions that make me ponder my worth. It only takes a few minutes and in those few minutes I'm transformed from a retiring yet confident individual into a self-centred egomaniac out of touch with reality. I don't feel any different but my new friend assures me it's all there in the way I've answered the questions. The form confirms it: my life's a crock.

It's that bad, huh? What can I do?

Fear not, hope is at hand. I can reach my full potential, become a better person, find untold wealth, be attractive to the opposite sex and live forever if I answer a few more questions. All I have to do is follow the Street Interrogator up some stairs and into a grey office.

It concerns me that the good folk asking the questions always seem more in need of guidance than anyone they stop. If this person has found their 'full potential' why isn't there any physical evidence? Why are they dribbling out of both sides of their mouth at once? And if this is an improvement, what were they like before? It's wrong to judge a book by its cover but these are people we're talking about. Grey gabardine shorts, white socks pulled up to his knees, greasy hair plastered flat on one side of his balding pate and he's asking me if *I* need help? Hey, physician save yourself! Or the gibbering 18-year-old recruit fresh from Stupidville, whose face is still settling, telling you they can assist you. The only way they could assist is if they were asking, 'You want fries with that?' And yet you stand there smiling in the middle of a busy street while they tell you what a mess you've made of your life. (Too goddamn polite.)

There is a way you can take your revenge if you have a little time and don't care about your personality.[1] Your agenda is to have fun. Lure the SI towards you. You accomplish this by one of three methods:

1. the limping seagull method
2. the uncontrolled emotions method

3. the heaps of stinking cash sticking out of your pocket method.

Your mission, should you choose to accept it, is to get asked to do the big test.

When the big test is in front of you I have always found it's best to take a surreal approach. Circle at least two answers for every multiple choice, swap the test with your friends, leave entire sections out or ask if you can finish it at home in your own time. If a moral dilemma has an obvious answer find the most grotesque, inhuman response and circle that:

Consider the following question: a young, attractive family of four are involved in a high-speed collision with a tree. The expensive car is about to burst into flame. Do you

1. immediately ring the police and ambulance service?
2. without thinking of your own safety rush into the burning wreck and save lives?
3. wait for the fire to die down, get rid of the bodies, and sell the car for scrap?

The humane response is No. 1. I would mark No. 3 (with the proviso that I would also flog their still-smouldering body parts on the lucrative overseas organ market). You would be surprised how highly you can score as a motivated personality by this method. At the conclusion of the test a graph is made of your responses. This graph usually confirms that, yes, your life is a crock.

Although I have been very critical of methods employed by SIs, their carefully designed forms do help you uncover aspects of your personality. For instance, if you walk up the stairs, you've discovered – you're Gullible. If you sign away your earthly belongings for a 'seminar', you've discovered – you're Stupid. How much else you learn is up to you.

---

1. When I was a young man in Canberra I engaged in the sport of Street Interrogator baiting. I now realise it was wrong and I regret doing it and would never suggest that it's a fun way to spend an afternoon with a couple of friends if you don't have any money and just want to annoy the crap out of people you don't know and will never see again (as long as you avoid that particular street).

The Heart of the Capital

I recently visited Canberra and recalled an incident that occurred when I lived there. It was something that made me realise that to find what you want, you have to know what you're looking for.

I once lived in a government bedsit on the main road into the city: Northbourne Avenue – a mighty six-lane river of bitumen that flowed into and out of this thriving metropolis. This primary road carried humanity, essential goods and livestock to feed the ever-expanding and insatiable community. (To be honest, most of the time there was nothing much on that road, with two exceptions: the ambulance that regularly passed by between 3 and 6 a.m. and always woke me up, and the Summer Nats.)[1]

The story I am about to tell you happened in early spring, on a Sunday, many years ago. I was enjoying the twenty-minute stroll from my squalid flat into town. It was a beautiful day, a typical Canberra spring day: sharp, teasing air, the rich scent of eucalyptus perfuming empty streets, the luminous yellow spray of wattle – all beneath a perfect canopy of cloudless pale blue.

There was nothing that could have shattered the serenity of that day. Even the occasional kamikaze magpie couldn't dent my spirit.

A car pulled up beside me.[2] An American voice beckoned me to the vehicle. Four travellers with a love of Australia had taken the journey overland to the ACT Three to four hours' driving through the bush may not seem like much to us, but to a group of Americans fresh out of New York it was exhausting. Their only desire was to see the city and find some accommodation. My heart surged with pride: here was my chance to give back a little something to the capital. I felt honoured to tell these people where to go.

'So where's the centre of town?'

'Straight ahead, you can't miss it, about three or four minutes in the car, mate.'

'Thanks, buddy.'

And they left. The only car on the road disappeared in a shimmering haze and the only person in the street waved them off.

Two hours later I was returning home on the other side of the same stretch of road, when a car pulled up next to me. It was the same hire car that had stopped me before. I had this curious sense of déjà vu when I heard: 'Hey buddy, where's the centre of town?' (It was a moment before they realised that I was the same person that had given them directions hours ago.) 'Hey, aren't you the same . . .'

'Yes. Didn't you find it?'

'We've been driving for two-and-a-half hours.' (They looked drawn, worn out and genuinely dizzy from the roundabouts.)

'Where have you been?'

'We went to somewhere called "Wooden".'

' "Wooden"?'

' "Wooden"!'

'Woden.'

'Whatever. We did what you said, we drove for about five minutes and we didn't see any tall buildings, so we kept going. Twenty minutes later – Wooden.'

'You won't find the centre of Canberra if you're looking for tall buildings.' (I explained to them the centre of town was just off a set of two-storey-high arcades and a bus depot.) 'If you turn to your left you'll find a police booth and a toilet block, and that's pretty much it.'

They'd missed the heart of our capital, not once but twice. They'd missed the eloquent designs of W.B. Griffin, the seat of power, the burgeoning porn industry and Bunda Street where the junkies hang out. When they set off for the third time, they were sincerely depressed. I have no idea if they found it, all I know is I never saw them again. They may still be there, endlessly looping around Northbourne Avenue like a malfunctioning satellite.

Canberra is often accused of having no heart; I have never believed this to be true. It may have a weak pulse, but it's there. In a place that's a mass of contradictions perhaps we just need a few more signs, and people from out-of-town should definitely buy a map. But the best preparation of all is knowing what you'll find when you get there. So if you ever go searching for the heart of Canberra, make sure you don't have New York in your mind's eye.

1. At 'Nats' time the entire strip became crowded with every type of car and every type of facial hair known to 'man'. The Nats were a male thing, although seldom a *lone* male thing: the men tended to travel in packs or in smaller groups with their offspring. Families pushing strollers drank down sweet exhaust fumes from cars that were inspired by Big Daddy Roth cartoons. All Canberrans, from alphas to deltas, united to praise these deformed beasts of the street, these noble chariots of the highway.

2. It may be of some interest to note that there is now an Information Centre where the car stopped.

On the Wider Ramifications

of Choice

We are faced with a complex and distressing dilemma in the modern age: we have too many choices. In our blind quest for ultimate freedom we have placed our daily liberty in jeopardy. Every day we are forced to make decisions; they range from the mind-bogglingly difficult to the blindingly simple. As the world contracts about us it has become far denser, far more impractical. We are inundated by information, overcome by difference and baffled by variety. I believe we have reached a point where we must make a decision about making decisions or we may reach a point where the decision-making process is all we are capable of.

The full terror of what the future holds was hammered home when I attempted to order breakfast at a common cafe. My request was simple enough: bacon and eggs on toast, a pot of tea and orange juice. The conversation that followed left me dazed, confused and unable to eat.

'How do you want the bacon?'[1]

I thought this was a trick question and without meaning to be rude replied, 'Cooked . . .'

The waitress stared at me with lifeless eyes. I suspect she made a quick and unjustified character assessment as she mumbled under her breath something that sounded like 'arsehole'.

'Do you want it streaky, crispy, rindless, heavy on the fat, grilled or fried?'

Bacon had always been bacon to me. There was no great mystery: you asked for it and it arrived. A strip of pig nestled beside the unborn embryos of chickens, was that too much to ask for?

'Eggs? Sunny side up, over easy, runny, fried, poached, scrambled, hard-boiled, free range or battery?'

I couldn't cope. I grabbed at the last word I heard. As it spluttered from my mouth I realised, too late, I shouldn't have said 'battery'. The other customers stopped eating and peered at me in disgust. A sweat formed on my brow. I had become, in an instant, a social pariah. I needed to catch my breath. I have never suffered asthma but I wanted a blast of Ventolin. The waitress had me on the ropes: she could see the fear in my eyes and she continued, in her merciless fashion, to destroy me.

'Toast? White, vitamin-enriched hi-energy white, brown, rye, sourdough, multigrain, yeast free, pumpernickel, Turkish, organic?'

I was bombarded by words. I could feel their weight upon me. I was crushed beneath them. She turned her attention to the tea.

'English breakfast, Earl Grey, Queen Mary, Russian caravan, jasmine, apple and citrus, fennel, rosehip, chamomile, peppermint, tannin-free or green?'

Adrenaline pumped into my veins; I could hear my heart-beat as a dull thud in the centre of my body.

'Freshly squeezed orange juice or the other stuff?'

I could sense her readying for the kill but for some reason she took pity on me and moved slowly away from the table.

My inability to deal with the situation made me acutely aware of other, similar circumstances where multiplicity has made life difficult. Remember when Band-Aids came in one multipurpose shape? When there were only two car companies to choose from? When the only pasta was spaghetti? Once everyone had the same haircut, listened to the same music, wore the same clothes, ate the same food and genuinely enjoyed life. Then war came along and ruined everything. Men and women fought bravely for our freedom to choose, but they didn't have to contend with hundreds of different mobile phone plans.

We live in a world with a myriad of possibilities and the emotional pressure this places on the individual is enormous. This may be the reason why High Court judges, and other people in positions of power, abdicate their responsibility and choose to wear diapers and be fed baby food. In that warm cocoon of well-financed care they make no decisions, feel no pressure and escape the rigours of modern life.

In the near future we must make the choice for less choice, we must decide to be indecisive, curtail our ever-expanding freedom and recover our liberty. Choice has always been promoted as a good thing, but anyone knows that a difficult decision can cause a great amount of distress. How much unnecessary anguish do we endure each and every day?

By the time the food arrived I had lost my appetite, but the waitress had one more surprise in store for me. A maniacal grin crossed her face.

'What type of milk do what with your tea? Full-cream, skim, calcium-enriched, iron-enriched, soy, lo-fat or chocolate?'

---

1. I confess that I am an eater of meat. I have tried over the years to acquire a taste for vegetables and fruit but I have always failed. I understand why vegetarian groups cry, 'Meat is murder.' I agree with them, but there is something so damn satisfying about consuming a beast that has died for you. It is tribal and instinctive: to stop its heart, ingest its soul, steal its spirit. I cannot imagine any similar joy in stealing the soul of a carrot.

Santa, the Jolly Thief

For once in my life I wanted to be the first at something and here it is. I wanted to be the modern equivalent of John the Baptist, preparing the way for the big fella who will follow. It won't be long now. It gets closer every year. Within a few weeks we'll see the tell-tale signs: pine trees on every corner, untold bargains, frosted windows, happy little faces, unconditional love. I wanted to be the first person this year to remind you that Christmas is just around the corner, so you'd better start saving now. I wanted to be the first person to raise the spectre of Santa Claus and the feelings of doubt.

Santa is a thief, a jolly red giant who steals every penny you save over the course of the year. Saint Nick and Ol' Nick have more in common than their names. Santa was never truly altruistic. His whole reputation is built on a lie. Having to leave biscuits and milk in exchange for the presents made him mercenary. As the years wore on the old sod developed a taste for beer and crackers. These offerings would always be gone by morning and when I multiplied our hospitality by the rest of the world it added up to a lot of beer and crackers. I pictured an out-of-control sleigh aquaplaning across the heavens as Santa tried to make it home before he was stopped by the big RBT in the sky. Santa is a dipsomaniac, a sozzle-pot: that would explain his permanently rosy cheeks and his gin-blossom nose.

I have bizarre recollections of my first encounter with this mythical man of mirth and girth. It occurred on a brilliantly hot December day. As the road melted we were told we were off to the North Pole. As the sweat poured from us we were led into an Arctic kingdom girt by airconditioners. In the middle of a drab mall we encountered the snow castle – a magical land of cardboard and white paint that wouldn't deceive a goat let alone a mature two-year-old child.

And there, sitting in exhausted majesty, was Santa, but something was awry, something amiss with this toy maker from the north. Perhaps it was the acrylic beard or the ill-fitting wig or the stray nasal hairs but this Santa just wasn't right. There was a massive gap between what I had imagined and the monstrosity of reality that confronted me. I couldn't put my finger on what it was that left me with a permanent loss of faith in Christmas. It may have been when he lifted me to his knee and revealed an overly hairy wrist and a tattoo. I assumed later it was a prison tattoo, completed in less than ideal conditions in the maximum-security wing, a faded bluebird with the word 'MABEL' frozen in a drunken ribbon. It may have been the potent smell of tobacco that filled my nostrils every time he spoke or the fact he burped as he asked me what I wanted 'on that special day'. I remember thinking, 'Santa's been eating a pie', as the atmosphere grew thick and meaty around us. I suppose it takes a special type of stamina and endurance to cope with a toddler's damp arse on your thigh all day. Apart from the offending odours he was honest and unsanitised, and if anything, he was just too human.

When I was leaving I noticed a pack of Marlboro in his boot. At least he managed to colour-coordinate his fags with his outfit. As I expected, I didn't get anything I asked for. Still I suppose a request for world peace was naive. (I was younger then; I realise now it's best to go for smaller, more manageable items.)

The idea of a big, jolly fat man distributing gifts, even from an early age, struck a chord of disbelief. It was enforced by the numerous and diverse shape-changing Santas. Every mall had one and every year they seemed to get younger. They were always surrounded by a cohort of dwarfs (occasionally made of wood) and accompanied by their faithful photographer. Because Santa appeared to be everywhere at the same time he took on a certain God-like quality. How could he ever live up to the image and the hype created for him?

My faith and trust in Santa was lost at an early age, in much the same way as was my trust in the economy, so I have come to warn you to be ready. When politicians make promises I am reminded of that wet knee. (You'd say anything to stop someone pissing on you.) Half the year has evaporated and most of us haven't prepared ourselves for the 'joys' of Christmas. It's been a good year so far: international financial disaster followed domestic financial disaster. How will you explain to those questioning little eyes that the dollar is worth less than spit and Santa might have to sell the reindeer? How will you tell them Father Christmas has been hard hit by the collapse of the Asian economies? We've been obsessed with interest rates, the fall of the dollar, the situation in Queensland, the federal election, the end of the financial year, the tax man knocking on our door, and we haven't spared a thought for 25 December. Just take a moment to let it all sink in and ruin your day.[1]

Maybe this is the year to spoil yourself and splurge on the beer and crackers now, while you can afford them.[2]

---

1. These closing comments are time-specific. However, as each year passes, it seems they are perennial dilemmas (especially Queensland).

2. I have always found the confusion and profusion of Christian and pagan imagery in the celebration of Christmas fascinating. If you have a perverse interest in this happy day that rejoices in the birth of Christ and sends ruddy-faced fat men down chimneys then several other pieces may appeal to you. These are 'The Approach of the Expected' (p. 158), 'The High Cost of Giving' (p. 161), 'The Death Clock' (p. 168), 'Holiday Hell' (p. 172) and 'The Last Time of Our Lives' (p. 183).

The Wonders of Body Language

When thoughts emerge from the mouth they are pure, straight from the mind and out into the world. However, once our speech is transposed into writing it has been corrupted: impositions of style and form have been placed upon it. Text is secondary to speech: it exists as a poor cousin to the profound moment of the word. Yet for all of its power it is still limited by our vocabulary. And no amount of words can capture the essence of a thought, which, like a perfect circle, may only exist in the mind. At the beginning of the 21st century the purest language we possess is still the language of the body.

Over the centuries our ability to understand each other in purely physical terms has been lost. The twisting facial expressions needed to communicate the operation of a pork mincer or a torque wrench are nothing compared to the amount of physical contortion necessary to convey the ideals of freedom, liberty or love.[1] Spoken language developed out of a need to express higher concepts. Then in the mid-seventies this skill was resurrected and we took our first awkward steps to overpower the written word.

All that was needed was keen observation to hone our animal instincts and strip away the facade of civilisation – to become primitive, natural, earthy. I admit that these early attempts were crude, focusing almost exclusively on the sex act. Body language was reduced to a series of signals, gimmicks, for attracting the opposite sex. A turn of the head, a flick of the hair: all simplistic mating gestures. It became another victim of the *me* generation, a sad charade played out at singles bars, a 'visible dialogue' fit only for wife-swapping[2] parties and advertising boardrooms.

The net result was that minders told politicians not to cover their mouths when they spoke in case they gave the impression they were lying, actors discovered how to convey emotion with their knees and alpha males learnt to 'spray' their environments to maintain control. What may have been the greatest achievement of humanity led to a few sordid encounters and mountains of useless publications.

At the close of the century we have become confused by the inarticulate speech of our body parts: sitting for hours pointing our feet towards someone hoping they will respond by turning their body slightly, or opening our lips in a 'moist, inviting way' only to find we look like an overfed goldfish, or saying 'no' with our mouth and 'yes' with our eyes.

Even with body language I still manage to get my foot stuck in my mouth. And if I can't hear what my body is telling me, how will I manage to listen to what other people's bodies are saying to me? And do I really want to? Everything I have heard from other bodies so far has been fairly grotesque, and more often than not, accompanied by foul and offensive odours. Some people are in tune with themselves – they know what their bodies need. I have no idea. Even if we spoke the same language it would be difficult enough, but over the years my body has developed a language all of its own with an obscure dialect and curious syntax that defies comprehension. When I watch myself I have no idea what I am saying.

In this modern age there is a schism between the body and the mind, a division in the natural order of things that forces us to go back if we want to move on. As we scream towards Armageddon, as conversation becomes more convoluted, sophisticated and dull, as technology fails to deliver the simplicity we need to return to what is pure, we need to listen to our bodies. The time has come to let our bodies speak for themselves, because if we keep sitting on our arses we may never hear what they have to say.

---

1. I am thinking here of Platonic love. Body language can easily express sexual need or desire; it may be as obvious as a grind of the hips or as subtle as a wink. I have witnessed all kinds of indecent and vulgar movement to express these feelings. It's a demeaning slang of our body tongue and is often accompanied by a guttural tone, a grunt or a whistle.

2. I first became aware of the term 'wife swapping' as an infant. My concern was caused by the fact that this expression was gender-specific. Surely the husbands were swapped at the same time as the wives, and yet no-one ever referred to 'husband swapping'. I have heard this barbaric practice continues in the more conservative suburbs and I am sure we have matured enough as a culture to let the little ladies have a rest and the fellas have a go. I also feel if women were swapping their husbands they would want something more practical than just another man.

The Call of the Siren

This was the perfect conclusion to an unspectacular day: a traffic jam. I surveyed the world from the car window. The glassy-eyed misery of every driver mirrored my own. We sat in unmoving lines of metal and rubber, spewing forth carbon monoxide from exhausts left to idle for hours. We had one thing in common, we all wanted to be somewhere else, but there we were, trapped, our lives wasting away to hits from the 'seventies, eighties and nineties'.

Then something inspiring happened. I heard it before I saw it, a clean beautiful machine ducking and weaving through the assembled throng. This car seemed to skate over the top of us. It showed no concern for road rules as it mounted the pavement. Terrified smaller cars bunched together helping it through, clumsy vehicles bumped fenders to get out of the way. I became aware of the hierarchy of the automobile. There I was trapped in a second-rate road muncher, a four-wheeled death trap, while what was akin to automotive royalty flew by. Its tail lights disappeared into the night and we were left to contemplate its passing.

We were stuck at the lights, our meagre lives dwindling

away, while this magnificent vehicle sped on, saving and savouring life. It had a graceful streamlined appearance, and sirens, and lights, and words written backwards on the hood. It was a sublime combination of form and function, the zenith of car manufacture, or to put it in layman's terms, a panel van with the lot.

We'd all get to where we were going a lot quicker if we drove ambulances. Ambulance drivers must get everything done they need to do; I'm envious of the time they must save. They'd be able to pay the bills, do the banking and make it from one side of town to the other even in rush hour. Nothing would stand in their way. Imagine just for one day having all that power and using it for your own selfish ends. An ambulance driver would never do anything untoward, but if these people have nothing to hide why are the windows always closed?[1]

I am, by nature, suspicious. If an ambulance passes me at the lights I have no idea if it's someone with a ruptured kidney being rushed to hospital or someone just rushing home to catch *Seinfeld*? I'm not so grim as to imagine that if the occupant was a geriatric having a cardiac arrest, a driver would whip down the shops and do a bit of grocery shopping (although there is plenty of room in the back of an ambulance, and if grandpop had a seizure he could also stop the pulp settling in the orange juice).

Everyone seems to be coming up with insane plans for saving this country at the moment, so here's another: it's a fairly radical idea but it could just work. I believe we should all drive ambulances. We should piss off every other car on the market and just make and sell ambulances. That way we could all get to where we're going, they'd be no traffic jams, and *free*ways would be just that. If we all had them maybe it would defeat the purpose, but just for a moment let's weigh up the pros and cons.

- On the negative side – there aren't as many seats in an ambulance.
- On the positive side – there is always somewhere comfy to lie down.
- On the negative side – the ambulance is quite difficult to park.
- On the positive side – you could probably leave it anyway as long as the lights were flashing. What sort of heartless creature would dare to give an ambulance a ticket?
- On the negative side – could get annoying if the kids are always playing with the sirens and the lights.
- On the positive side – you've got as much pure oxygen as you want, a whole pharmacy in the back, and you can check your blood pressure any time.
- On the negative side – with everyone ignoring the road rules, running reds, mounting the pavement, there'd be a lot more accidents.[2]
- On the positive side – there'd be a lot more ambulances on the road. There'd always be one around if you were in an accident. As a matter of fact, you'd be *in* one.

So I think I'll go out on a limb here and suggest that every car in this beautiful, brown country of ours be an ambulance. Hell, it makes as much sense as printing money.

---

1.   I would never suggest that an ambulance – a vehicle designed for a specific purpose – would be used for the personal gain of the driver. It just strikes me that we are all human and thus capable of acts of great

cruelty and stupidity. And placed in a similar situation I would not hesitate to use the machine for evil.

2.   I personally think the ambulance service does a wonderful and essential job and if I should be involved in some accident in the next few weeks I would trust that this flight of fancy would not be taken personally.

Smoking at the Start of

the Century

• Part 1

I t is the greatest tragedy this world has ever known. It has infiltrated every society, poisoned anyone it touched and polluted the world. Over the past few years Satan, Saddam and smoking have battled it out for the title of 'Ultimate Evil' but the big belt goes to the humble fag. The battle lines have been drawn between the 'Clean Lungs' and the 'Yellow Fingers', and the fate of the earth hangs in the balance.

What travesties of justice are committed when lighting up in a small office or having a puff while you're pregnant? Has an individual's space ever been more compromised than with the insidious creeping death of the cigarette? Who has not leant back after a fine meal, savouring the flavour of an expensive crème brûlée, only to have their senses overpowered by the noxious, invasive odour of a coffin stick? Who has ever had smoke blown in their face by an overachieving brain-dead freak of inferior moral and social standing? Who has ever witnessed a forty-five-year-old adolescent use their mouth as an ashtray and thought, 'Grow up!'?

In days long gone, smoking assured you a treasured place

in society, the constant affection of the opposite sex and riches beyond your wildest dreams. With a cigarette dangling from your lip you had the wisdom of Solomon, the wealth of Rockefeller and the sexual power of Valentino. Thankfully these images of smoking have decayed as quickly as our respiratory tracts. Nowadays you're as popular as O.J. Simpson, have pox-ridden lungs and the pity of all your friends. Graphic TV commercials depict clotted arteries and fat-strangled hearts and are usually screened for our edification around dinner time. As a sterile hand squeezes another hunk of ulcerated lard out of a bloated tube the innocent are turned off their meals and the smoker just turns the channel. What is achieved by these ads: you're throwing up your pasta and they're smoking in front of *The Simpsons*?

Despite Quit campaigns, family pressure, hypnosis and support networks the smoker continues to evade capture. The 'Yellow Fingers' will always succeed in the short term because they're cunning, clever and, more often than not, fun to be around. But there is a larger problem than the individual puffer and it is one few of us have recognised.

In our desire to banish smokers from polite society we have foolishly created a new underclass. You can see them huddled together at the back entrance of every department store, beneath enormous airconditioner ducts in public-service workplaces, a small, tireless band of men and women prepared to stand up to the tyranny of the politically correct. You tend to notice them more in the winter months when they're the only people milling about in the freezing cold. They're easy to recognise by the halos of smoke that ring their heads and their plaintive cry, 'Got a light? Got a light? Anyone got a light?' They are crowded together for support and warmth, and in between drags they even talk. This is the dilemma.

Once like-minded people from different offices would never meet, never converse, and the status quo was maintained. Now this offensive minority, who have spoilt it for years for all air-breathers, have the opportunity to rally their numbers and realise their demented, nicotine-fuelled dreams. In these haphazard meetings is it possible that alliances are formed? In the cold of winter, in the glow of Bic lighters, are plans being hatched? Is the terror within actually just fagging-on outside? Having one of them in an office was easy enough to handle – they could be ostracised during morning tea, marginalised by management and overlooked for promotion. There were numerous ways to keep them at bay. But now that they're organised they just need the right catalyst to burn out of control.[1]

In America there are now all-smoking aircraft where even the pilots enjoy a mild twenty-five before take-off. Restaurants, cinemas, nurseries and churches: nothing is beyond their power to control. Forced segregation has mobilised them into a political force – one that transcends race, colour, creed, weight and gender boundaries. How long before this beautiful land falls prey to the ashtray apartheid?

For too long we, the 'Clean Lungs', have tolerated their foul breath, their claustrophobic clouds of cancer, their dirty teeth and stained nails. We have tolerated the fact that they look cool, in a nonchalant sort of way that can only be accomplished with a cigarette. We have loathed how they always have something to do with their hands. But can we face a world where accidental meetings give them an edge? In a cliché of justifiable paranoia, 'Keep your friends close, but your enemies closer.' It may be time to invite smokers in from the cold, at least until we know what their master plan is.

---

1. This is just a provocative phrase, and I'm not suggesting that smokers are arsonists, but if we're being honest, they are the ones with the matches.

Smoking at the Start of

the Century

• Part 2

S hakespeare once wrote in praise of tobacco, 'O thou weed,/Who art so lovely fair, and smell'st so sweet . . .'[1] Over the centuries great poets, writers and artists have been inspired by 'sublime tobacco', but these days there is a perception that smoking is not merely misguided but evil. At the risk of being savaged by the politically correct, the surgeon general and conscientious families I intent to defend the right to smoke. It is important that we understand smoking in its historical context and not just as a product subjected to years of hyperbole and discrimination.

There is little doubt that smoking has had a chequered career; it has been loathed and despised as much as it has been loved. From the moment humanity conquered fire and someone thought 'That looks dangerous – I wonder if I could suck it into my body', smoking has been a contentious issue. It has dominated politics, been incorporated into religious ceremonies, and featured in great literature and art. And it was the peace pipe that made smoking the embodiment of an ideal.

Smoking the peace pipe: a symbolic gesture of unity and

fellowship that could easily make the uninitiated feel nauseated and dizzy. This traditional method of seeking accord has echoes in many cultures, although it is attributed primarily to the Native American. One has only to look at the relationship that exists between the government of that 'great union' America and its indigenous population to see how marvellously effective this process can be.

We have only to look at the work of The Rolling Stones to see how attitudes have changed over the years. In the classic tune of angst-ridden alienation, 'Satisfaction', Mick Jagger sings that only those who smoke his brand are real men. This is a damning indictment from the coolest dude in drawstring trousers. Forty years after this track was recorded the Stones album *Pushing It Uphill* features a heavy-handed antismoking message. On the track 'Don't Smoke, It's Bad for You', Mr Jagger coughs his way through three verses of propaganda while Jerry asks Keith to put it out when the kids are around.

There was a time when the humble cigarette was our friend, before it became the prime suspect in the hunt for the 'big C'. It was on a hookah that the caterpillar puffed as he spoke to Alice and thus an endearing children's character was born. In these more enlightened times would we ever allow Dipsy or Po to reach for a Longbeach? Will the Bananas ever light up? And is it mere coincidence or the work of a politically correct conspiracy that Bill Steamshovel seems to have disappeared? Up until recently films featured good men and women with the 'filthy habit'. These fine troubadours, many now riddled with cancer, championed the cause of the cigarette. Once cowboys wore white hats and blew smoke rings as they saved the innocent, detectives savoured the flavour solving hideous crimes and lovers shared a post-coital moment with a puff. These days no decent human being on the big or small screen smokes and you're only permitted to inhale if you're a killer, a thief or poorly educated – the good guys don't smoke, which is something the image-makers know only too well.

Anyone with political aspirations understands that smoking is taboo and being caught with a fag can destroy your career. If these attitudes had prevailed fifty years ago, the world could be a very different place today. Winston Churchill, the cigar-chomping hero of World War II, wouldn't have lasted two minutes on the political stage before being pulled down by well-meaning, socially aware, smoke-intolerant lobbyists. No amount of support from the tobacco industry would've saved him from the indignation of the populace, and the world would've lost a powerful and inspirational leader. During those years of war young heroes huddled together prior to a moment of truth. In those precious moments before going 'over the top' to certain death those brave lads were unified by the chemical wonder of the American tobacco industry. Who recalls the stirring cry of the sergeant, 'Smoke 'em if you got 'em'? Is it too much to suggest that without the leadership of Winston Churchill or the tailor-made troops we might be breathing clean air under a fascist regime?

What does the future hold? There'll be no more wheezing politicians, no more lovable children's characters with bad habits, no more poets and playwrights composing odes to the ashtrays. And in the event of a terrible war there'll be a last glass of milk before you go over the top – and let's face it, that just doesn't cut it. There are many positive aspects to smoking that are not immediately apparent to the naked eye, in the same way that many of the negative aspects cannot be seen without X-rays, CAT scans or taking bits of skin off to be analysed. We live in a society fractured by divisions – can we allow another to exist between smokers and nonsmokers? Has the time come for all of us to sit down and smoke the pipe of peace?

---

1. This line from *Othello* is directed towards Desdemona. Almost all Shakespearean scholars maintain that she is the 'weed' in question. I've done no research on this topic but feel well within my rights to challenge them on this assumption. I personally feel that the bard is being annoyingly literal on this occasion.

    It is fair to assume that at the time he was oblivious to the carcinogenic qualities of 'the weed'.

Standardisation and Repetition

The world isn't only getting smaller, it's getting similar. Everything is becoming standard. The wonderful diversity that we once rejoiced in is being modified, watered down, digested and absorbed. The books we read are full of the same words, the films we see are full of the same actors, and the songs we hear are full of the same sounds. There are international bodies attempting to standardise everything we eat, drink and breathe. We are becoming a generic people in a no-name world stuck in a brand-less universe.

In Japan there's a theme park, and for the price of admission you can literally have the world at your feet. Every major city, architectural feat and natural phenomenon is represented in fibreglass and paint, shrunk to a photograph-friendly size. You can stand alongside a miniature Eiffel Tower, Big Ben or Opera House, you can marvel at a petite Rio Grande, dwarf the Victoria Falls and step over Uluru. You can travel the world in four hours and see all the 'major sights' without leaving the park. More importantly you can do all this and never have to fumble with a foreign currency, understand an exotic language, deal with the locals or catch a cab or dysentery.

Where the Japanese have made a little world in their backyard, Americans have done the opposite: their backyard is our little world. You can go anywhere across the globe and get the same burger and French fries, stay in the same room of the same hotel and watch the same TV shows. Incidentally, with cable you can watch the same shows from thirty years ago.

We all share a desire to remain within our comfort zone, an understandable need for the familiar, to dine on recognisable food, to be pampered by the usual. We feel safe and secure surrounded by the everyday, but it also limits our experience and could conceivably lead us to question the very nature of our existence. Sameness can now span generations.

Recently I overheard a tale that relates to the effect of the perpetually similar. The story concerns one Yusef Islam when he was still Cat Stevens. I presume this incident occurred before Cat embraced Allah and called for the death of Salman Rushdie, and I'm not suggesting the two are connected.

In the mid-seventies Cat was still a wandering minstrel packing them in to sell-out stadium shows across the States. Tired and confused by constant travel Cat became convinced that he wasn't moving at all.[1] He would arrive in a new town that looked exactly like the town he had just left and head straight to the new hotel, which looked exactly the same as the last hotel. After a while the repetition got to him, and he believed that he was stationary and the world was being rotated around him. He convinced himself that he was staying in the same hotel every day and that all the travelling, the shows, the little towns, the people were part of a conspiratorial plot to drive him insane. He fought the feelings for as long as he could and then, not being able to stand it any longer, he decided to test his theory.

He wrote his name on a part of the wall hidden by the bathroom mirror. When he arrived at the next town he would check behind the mirror, there would be nothing there, and his instability would evaporate. Unfortunately for the fragile mind-set of Mr Stevens he had been observed by one of his crew. The roadie checked to see what had been written, gauged the situation and decided to have some fun. Arriving at the next town before Cat he copied the 'soon to be unhinged' one's child-like scrawl on the wall covered by the mirror. When Cat cruised into the bathroom he fully expected to rid himself of his paranoia; instead he saw his name – CAT. Worlds collided and he caught the first train to Loopyville, a crazy fruitcake Fantasy Land of full-steam-ahead delusional madness.[2]

In the not too distant future we may all become like Cat. I don't mean we'll all become Muslim – although that's not a bad thing in itself – but we may find ourselves in a world devoid of difference. A place where global standards mean we're all safe, secure and the same; where all sound has been blended to form a hideous white noise and all colour combined to form a murky grey. And in this place where everything is equal we might begin to crave the difference and diversity we have lost. We may all, like Cat, pray that we don't see the writing on the wall, behind the bathroom mirror.

---

1. I have no idea if Cat was a lean, clean music machine and refrained from imbibing illegal stimulants. However, I would suggest a certain

amount of recreational drug use would create the perfect atmosphere from which to springboard into dementia.

2. It's a tragedy that all practical jokes are not this effective; most are pathetic attention-seeking devices.

The Unseen Dangers
of Water

I n the dark days since the crisis began[1] we have all tried to find a way through, a way to survive. My way, though unconventional, has achieved surprisingly beneficial results. Vodka, straight up, looks almost the same as water and I have managed to convince myself it is. All alcohol is a depressant, but then no more depressing than the state of our water. Over the last few weeks I have used vodka[2] as a substitute for all my needs, immersing myself in its antiseptic medicinal wonder and guzzling its grandeur. I have stopped bathing. I believe the cryptosporidium can find other ways into my body. I still maintain a rigorous regime of cleansing, sponging daily with a mixture of pure alcohol (vodka) and a splash of cooking sherry.

I learnt to adapt early. On the first day of the emergency I took every opportunity to fill my mouth with rancid-stinking-bacteria-ridden Sydney water. I woke up and brushed my teeth. I absent-mindedly swallowed the residue and gunk in my mouth – a curious mix of tasty menthol and microorganisms. When I remembered why I hadn't brushed the night before, the horrible realisation struck and I immediately tried to rinse my

mouth out with the same poisoned tap water. Over the course
of the day I kept drinking the stuff like it was going out of style –
mixing it with cordial, something I normally never touch. Months
into this man-made disaster I stumble into the bathroom with
groggy, pus-crusted eyes and only manage to avert disaster with
the trusty vodka.

How did this happen in 'Australia's most beautiful city'?
Conspiracy theories abound: there are no bacteria – it is a plan
by the government to save water for the Olympics; jealous Vic-
torians released the parasites into the reservoir; it's a way of
diverting attention from the election; we're in a drought situation
and no-one ever listens when they're asked 'nicely' to conserve;
politically motivated hippies from Byron dropped lysergic acid in
the dam and the government wants it all for themselves; a
mineral water company needed a way to up sales. The list goes
on, and as scientists debate the real danger to the populace we
are left to be mocked and ridiculed by the other states.

For many of us this is the greatest indignity: to be humiliated
before the nation. Over the centuries the rest of the country has
wanted a reason to pull Sydney down, to drag this majestic town
to their gutter level and now they have it – a tainted cup, poured
by our own hand and stirred by our own stupidity.

The shame and embarrassment: more than any other aspect,
that has become impossible to handle. The minor states are revel-
ling in our demise and the rest of the world is watching: CNN,
Associated Press and British television have all had a jolly good
laugh at our expense. Melbourne, if it need be said, is overjoyed,
Perth sees it as further evidence of the decline of the East and
Adelaide wants to bottle our water and sell it. The indignity
would have been enough to last a lifetime even if the tragedy

had only spanned a week. If only the authorities had fished out the 'dead dog' and that had been the end of it. But no, the population seesawed on conflicting and baffling information – 'it's safe', 'it's not safe', 'it's safe again', 'it's over', 'it's not'. It's not over and for many of us it never will be. Melbourne may well be the 'anus of the world' but Sydneysiders are drinking from it.[3]

When it finally ends, will it really be over? Can we ever look at our taps in the same way again? Will we always be asking, 'Is it safe?' The one thing we can rely on is the indomitable human spirit. We will find a way through this together and we will come out the other side. Let us not forget: that which does not kill us makes us stronger. Unless, of course, we just get a tummy bug, excruciating stomach cramps and diarrhoea that lays us low for a week or two but has no discernible effect on our spirit or mentality.

---

1. See 'The Olympics' (p. 88) for more details.

2. One of the other benefits of exchanging vodka for water is the amazing diversity of the alcoholic beverage. There's pepper, chilli, blackcurrant and some lovely citron flavours as well. It also gets you pissed, which water rarely does.

3. If the 'Very Fast Train' were here there would be no crisis. It is, after all, a short trip to Canberra for some of the finest tap water in the world. Then the capital city could have a water-shortage crisis. Incidentally, never trust the ice.

CONCERNING RITUAL

Your Resolve

How many weeks is it since you made that tortured promise? How many nights have you woken in a cold sweat, your boiling eyes dragging you from some new and hideous nightmare? How many times have you gone over the impassioned speech that condemned you to this unmitigated sadness? As the months pass by, and the rosy veil of stupidity is lifted from your mind, you realise how desperately dumb it was to make a new year's resolution.

The reason we make these promises on the eve of a new year has nothing to do with the hope and hidden promise of what is to come. It is based solely on the fact that at any other time of the year no-one would be gullible enough to do something so idiotic. Were you over-stuffed with Christmas joy or full to the brim with ale, eager to make an impression or convinced change was necessary? Was it at the bustling dinner table or whispered in the sanctuary of the bedroom? As everyone else shuffled out of the old year, as they congratulated you and patted your back, they were oblivious to the little black cloud of misery you'd tied to your head. Since that ground-breaking foolishness you've been searching for something to release you. Here it is: the three areas you must address in order to break the promise.

Personal

To make a resolution suggests that there is something about you that is wrong, vulgar, unattractive, odious, belligerent, crass, objectionable and yet somehow . . . redeemable. You are placed in the unenviable position of admitting to a character flaw or personality trait that you can rectify. It's never enough to say you'll fix it, it has to be seen to be fixed. For a resolution to be complete it must be witnessed. And there's the problem: we're obsessed with magnanimous gestures and god-like goals that we can never hope to achieve. Resolutions should be human and shallow, like ourselves: I vow to be more attractive, or more popular, or dress to the left; in the coming year I promise to eat less dog food, not chase the elderly, be pleasant when I can be bothered.

If we allow our evil nature to dominate, the resolution will be a thing of self-destructive joy: I promise to be hedonistic, to be obsessive, to gamble, to drink excessively, to smoke until my cancered colon is ripped from my body.

When you realise your objective is unattainable, you're ready for the next step.

Emotional

We rarely, if ever, change to suit ourselves. We do it to accommodate others. There's a tenet you can live your life by that ensures the peer pressure involved in making a resolution becomes a thing of the past. It's a simple and dignified mantra that you can chant in front of a mirror, or if the need arises, it can be spoken aloud: I'm okay, you're stuffed!

Once you have decided to solve the dilemma of your resolution by bringing it to a premature end, you may need the support of your family and friends. If you can't break a promise to those closest to you, who can you break a promise to? It's difficult to stand up and proudly proclaim that you're weak and you lied. At the same time, once it's done, it's done. The onus then falls on whoever cares to accept it or not. If they do, the time is ripe to make other confessions: I assassinated the Arch-Duke Ferdinand, the Marconi scandal was my fault, I encouraged Burke and Wills on their fateful trip. While they're stunned into silence by your conversion to the truth, you could take the opportunity to mention all the failed resolutions from years gone by.

Legal

No court in the land could prosecute you for having failed to deliver on a new year's resolution, so legally speaking you're in the clear.[1] If it ever made it to the courthouse there are dozens of reasons why your promise could be considered invalid: you were adversely affected by the altruism of the evening and rendered momentarily insane; you were swept along with the mob mentality of a group of bare-arsed trumpet-blowing revellers; you were face down in a mass of someone else's stomach lining with a yard glass fused to your lips as you threw up your resolution.

———

In the end you can't change who you are. The sun and moon are chained to their course and birds flock together: there is no escape. It's time to accept you're a deceitful pile of bacteria-ridden skin held together by ear wax and bad breath. If you were capable of being a better person you would be already. So this year, if you haven't resolved to do so already, resolve to never make another resolution. They say you're only as good as your word, but then they're the ones smart enough to keep their mouths shut.

---

1.   Unless your resolution contravenes the laws of the land (e.g. 'Break out of prison before March').

The Approach of the Expected

The warning tremors are here already. There is a heightened sense of terror on the street. The desperate scramble has begun and it will not be over until well into the new year. Statistically more people suffer breakdowns during holidays, and Christmas takes the honours for the highest incidence of crack-ups. If your trolley is going to run off the rails, it is more likely to do so at Christmas time than at any other time of year. I am not telling you this to fill you with fear but so you can prepare for the trauma ahead. You are the most important person in the world, and for once, you must think of yourself. You're like Santa to your family: without you there is no yuletide joy. You are the passport to fun, the decorator of the tree, the wrapper of presents, the source of all understanding.

Don't expect your family to notice you falling apart. They're too busy trying to buy you presents. It is one of the great riddles of Christmas that we are so concerned with being generous we have very little time for kindness. You could be wearing a tutu, urinating into the salad, and no-one would notice.

You have worked hard this year and you deserve a rest. The

days grow shorter as your list of commitments grows longer. A few more hurdles and the end of the year is in sight. On the horizon a golden crest of glorious sunshine beckons. Christmas is coming and another year is condemned to memory. The time has come to let the sun kiss away the tears of anguish and to dance upon the edge of rainbows. I tell you: Don't Be A Fool! You are like a character in a film who has been bitten by a snake and just wants to lie down. But I am standing by your shoulder telling you to stand up, walk around, do not rest – your life depends on it.[1]

You can't wind down. You have got to stay tense. No! You can't afford to be tense! Why? Because everyone relies on you. But the mere fact everyone relies on you makes you tense. Admit you're tense. You're that poor, sad-looking Christmas tree in the corner. Each piece of tinsel, each tiny wooden Santa, every colou-red ball, drags your branches ever lower. Overloaded with baubles, bound by flashing lights and unbalanced, you are about to topple into the middle of the lounge.

The reason we experience trauma over Christmas is that we believe we can relax. I tell you solemnly: Do Not Relax. The only way to avoid a fall is to convince yourself the hurdles will keep coming. When the last hurdle is in sight, conjure another in your mind. As you approach that one, imagine another. Keep this up for the rest of your life. There is one consolation in this method: you'll die young.

Stay alert! In every store Christmas carols attempt to lull you into a false sense of security. Beware! These songs are a rallying call to misery. You are salivating at the thought of turkey and cranberry sauce. It is a recipe for disaster. To protect yourself and your family you must continue to set yourself hurdles, and whatever else you do, do not relax. Trust me, because four days ago I relaxed, and three days ago the wheels fell off my trolley.

Three days ago the face that greeted me in the mirror was not my own. A hideous creature loomed before me. Two dark black bags dragged my eyes down to my cheeks. My cheeks had collapsed into my neck. My neck was hiding in my chest. My stubble was like sandpaper. I accidentally sprayed Baygon on my toothbrush. At every turn malevolent forces conspired against me. The bus was late so I took a cab. The cab driver didn't seem to be in the same city as me. I was sweating, my heart was grey from worry. It was failing in its sole function – to keep me alive until the festive season. The lift was out so I took the stairs. I had a continual headache. It was behind my eyeball threatening to push the pulsing orb out of the socket and onto my cheek. I know it isn't a tumour. It can't be. I haven't got time for a tumour. A six-by-six block of gyprock fell from the ceiling. There's a smell in the house I can't locate. Someone keeps calling at 4.23 in the morning. I have been urinating into my salad.

I type this letter with a pencil attached to my forehead at a major metropolitan hospital.

---

1. A cautionary note: The treatment I refer to for snake bite is taken from early American westerns. This method has been proved to be incorrect, as any movement of the limb will increase the circulation of poison throughout the vascular system. Contemporary wisdom suggests the limb be immobilised by the use of a splint. In the case of an arterial puncture a tourniquet may need to be applied. It is essential the tourniquet be released regularly to ensure that blood to the limbs does not become completely occluded. Merry Christmas.

The High Cost of Giving

That joyous time is here again. That time of peace on earth and goodwill to all men[1] and universal happiness and unbridled greed. Just a few more days to discover how much you are loved. It is unrealistic to equate emotion with expenditure but it is something we all do. As the presents spiral outward from the tree our minds are engaged in mathematical gymnastics. How much was that? Where was it found? Were there many others like it? At Christmas there are numerical equations that indicate how much you are cared for, how much you are loved. The cost of the item (gift) over the income of the giver (approx.) multiplied by the amount of time spent searching is equal to the sum of their affection. With certain items – say a pair of pyjamas – I wouldn't even bother with the maths.

Christmas is a terrifying time when we tread a tightrope between loss and gain, love and hate. It is a time of judgement and reassessment. It is a time of defining ourselves in relation to others, and we do this by comparing – comparing what we got to what they got. You gave a state-of-the-art handmade juicer from Düsseldorf that took two weeks to find, she gave a pair of nylon-mix socks from Target. The juicer was $628, less $2.50 for the socks – that comes to a loss of $625.50. It is an awkward situation but just as awkward the other way around. If you're the receiver, you're suddenly aware that the giver has greater regard for you than you previously thought. You should also be aware that the giver is simultaneously discovering, as they rip open the wrapping of a bargain-basement CD of seventies love songs[2] you picked up at a newsagent, that you couldn't give a toss about them.

It is a time for questions. How many items of rubbish can I grab at the $2 shop, put in a box and send to the relatives I never see to make it appear I care? Can I make a family of five happy for $10 including postage?

And though you are loath to admit it, it is a time for getting what you want. In the months preceding the big day you've hinted at the perfect gift. You thought you were subtle, casually dropping the name of the object into every conversation for the last three months. You discussed your favourite colour, left notes on the fridge. When the ad appeared on TV you fainted with desire. If you had written it in blood on your forehead it couldn't have been more obvious.

Then the moment of truth arrives when you tear away the wrapping paper and the gift is not quite what you were expecting. The look of sadness that slurries across your face is impossible to disguise: that pretence of a smile curling into a sneer, the moisture in the corner of your eyes, that interminable silence as the room waits on your reaction and there is only one response you can ever make. 'I love it! WOW! Who would have thought of that as a present? A batik handbag and a plastic folding straw-look sunhat! Only you Nan, only you could have got me that.'

And thanks for the book on the Don but it was a bike I wanted. A bike! Because you can't ride a book to the park. And thanks for the no-name stretch stonewash flared cuff copy-cat jeans you picked up from a market at a bargain price because they're ten years out of date and have the crotch sown on backwards.

Even when we are given the options of an easy out we fail to take them. How often have you stood there inanely smiling while a distant voice says, 'If it doesn't fit you can take it back, or swap it for something you like'? You want to be honest but you find yourself lying. 'No, it looks great on me!' You long to say, in as gentle a way as possible, 'It's the wrong colour, the wrong size. I hate it! Get me something decent! I don't care if it's 11 a.m. on Christmas Day. Take it back! How could you think, even in your most deluded fantasy, that I would think that thing is attractive?' Your mind is screaming, 'It's crap!' But the words that dribble out of your mouth are, 'No, No, it's fine. It'll stretch.'

With all this talk about buying presents and the cost of giving, you may think I have lost the Christmas spirit. You may think I have forgotten the true meaning of the festive season. And you're right, Christmas is not about buying things, it's about selling them and selling them at outlandishly high prices.

An offensive afterthought: how many times have you purchased something for someone else because *you* loved it? You saw it and you wanted it but you gave it to someone you loved. And you gave it to them because you thought that you would be together forever and the good thing you gave them, that you loved, would be near you because you were with them. Then they decided they didn't love you and convinced you you didn't love them, but they still got the good thing that you managed to get, and they've still got it. And they're not going to give it to you. And every time you visit them (which is unsettling because once you believed you loved them and now you don't even like them) you see the good thing, the good thing that you wanted but you gave away, and merely seeing it again makes you slightly nauseated.

1. This is a sadly archaic phrase that does not extend 'goodwill' to all our sisters.
2. Not by the original artists.

On New Year's Eve

Have you looked in the mirror lately? You look haggard! Not just haggard but a year older, as if a year passed last night and left you in its wake. So do not look in the mirror.

It is time to take stock of the year. To look over the past year with all its ups and downs, highs and lows, and set about cataloguing events. Before you engage in that gruesome task, you have to run the gauntlet: the end-of-year office parties culminating in the terrifying New Year's Eve bash. In regard to parties, there is no more dangerous time of year. They can make or break you socially so it is essential you pace yourself. An early dash, though much admired, could leave you drained and unable to be the star attraction at the big one. The big one should always be your focus. Never lose sight of that ball falling in New York, the sheer joy, the excitement, the countdown; and if you're not there the next day you won't be able to forget what you don't want to remember from the previous night.

Hopefully by now you will have completed the obligatory office functions. The ones you say you hate ('It's work, they expect me. I get no enjoyment out of this either! This is a no-fun zone for me too you know!') and every year there you are. At some point in the evening you look around to find the sedate world you inhabit during the week has gone out of control. In one corner men and women in party hats enact scenes from Sodom and Gomorrah with photocopiers taking the place of goats. Mrs Somebody, a simmering cauldron of repressed sexuality, is dancing lasciviously with a gawky, angular, post-baby-boomer on a co-worker's desk. You drink a glass of water that someone has ashed in and come to the conclusion that all water is bad for you. The teetotallers are consuming the most alcohol, the 'quiet ones' are talking your ear off and the girl that 'always has a smile on her face' is crying in the corner. A conversation a year in the making is occurring, the protagonists are shocked, but everyone else is glad it's finally happened. The guy everyone hates breaks down and says he's sorry and the office forgives him, for a second, until they regroup and recall what an arsehole he is. You catch a glimpse of yourself in a darkened window but manage to turn away before any real damage is done. As you leave you find yourself saying in all honesty, 'What a great night! Hope it's as good next year!'

Then the big one – New Year's Eve. In one swift act of purging we rid ourselves of the old skin of the fading year and prepare to snuggle into the soft skin of the new. We normally manage to do this by staying up all night and losing any sense of decency. Old Father Time bows out and the Child of Time, fresh from the crib, is already ageing rapidly.

We manage to blot out this 'passing of time' with the convenient memory loss that overindulgence brings. We see the night as a disjointed series of events. There is never any coherent story, just one disaster after another. Spilled drinks, forgotten names, accidental meetings, lost friends, bad jokes that lead us in a dizzy rush to the countdown. Followed swiftly by the disgusting feeling of being kissed by total strangers on the stroke of midnight.[1] Or even worse, on the stroke of midnight being steadfastly avoided by total strangers. While everywhere around you people abandon themselves, you're left standing, lips untouched. The hours fly till dawn; when you come to, there are always streamers and confetti on the floor. A few days later you inevitably find something in your pocket. You don't know when it got there, or more importantly, how it got there, and you're too ashamed even to look at it. In the last twenty-four hours you've committed at least four of the seven deadly sins, which you can't remember enough to enjoy. You greet the first day of January in a darkened room because overnight you've become light-sensitive.

And, although you were warned, you look at yourself in a mirror and discover you have become a walking, talking, all-singing, all-dancing version of your own death. You're the monster from the bottom of the bottle coming up for air. As you peer into your eyes, the mirror of your soul, you see shattered glass and read 'You are truly alone' scratched into your retina. What I recommend is closing your eyes for a while and going to sleep because tonight . . .

---

1. The 'stroke of midnight' is not a euphemism.

The Death Clock

Two swallows raced past my window. They circled each other in dizzying spirals before returning to their nest. In the backyard flowers courted bees and two kittens tumbled together, blissful in their ageless play. Everywhere I looked there was new life: unbridled, robust and determined. It was a beautiful spring day when a close friend told me the hour of my death.

She had visited an Internet site that makes a calculation based on the average life expectancy. You type in your basic details and it gives you a date. What morbid fascination had drawn her to the site still eludes me. It also distressed me that her date for departure was a good thirty years after mine. She had thirty years to party on in the wonderful world of the future. The other unsettling aspect of the prediction was learning that I am destined to leave this earth sometime midmorning 25 December 2036.[1] I didn't want to abandon this ball of dust and spit. I didn't want to accept the fact that there was an end to all this sorrow and frivolity. In this day and age there's just too much to look forward to.

Our knowledge of ourselves has changed dramatically over the centuries. Especially our concept of age. Children are teenagers these days around the age of eight. The teenage years of wonder, narcissism and sexual exploration can last well into the twenties, while if you're determined, you can now make your twenties last until your fifties. In our times people are less inclined to be responsible. Our marriage and birth rates have declined as we tenaciously pursue fun. We're living longer and enjoying life more (and if we're not enjoying life as much as we could be, there's an awesome arsenal of antidepressants to cheer us up). Who wants it to stop? What other age has offered so much? How hellish would life have been before the invention of spectacles in 1303? And when we could see clearly, what was there to look forward to? The abolition of the Poll Tax (1381), radical advancements in pulleys, another bout of scurvy? In 1777 Dr Samuel Johnson said, 'When a man is tired of London, he is tired of life.' Yet it was proved by the Burton Society in 1857 that you could be tired of London in just under three weeks less if you had no money. Thus we arrive at the Victorian age, and now what is there to entice us? The last instalment of *Bleak House*? Seeing an ankle before you die? Inventing a new and fascinating way of eating a potato? Until the beginning of the 20th century life idled along from one generation to the next. Apart from the hem of women's skirts and facial hair on men, nothing much changed from one lifetime to another. In days gone by it must have been a pleasure to get your marching orders to the next world. Even in the technologically advanced West going to the toilet has only become an enjoyable experience in the past fifty years.

Over the centuries these discoveries have been fascinating,

but compared to the rate of change over the past 100 years they're nothing. Every day there are more questions. What will happen in the fields of biotechnology, genetic engineering and virology? What will *Voyager* discover beyond our solar system? Is there life elsewhere in the universe? Will we ever achieve a united peace for all peoples of all countries based on egalitarian systems of government, economic reform and decent TV? But these are the mere tip of the ideological iceberg. What about the eternal questions? Will Macaulay Culkin ever make a comeback? Will there be a *Notting Hill 2*? Will there be a solo album from all five members of Five? And how did they get their name? Will someone assassinate Jerry Springer? Will they ever legalise everything?

This is the worst age to be alive; give us the physical pain of the past, not the mental anguish of never knowing the answers. The future is here, now, tumbling around us constantly. We can no more stop it than we could stop the sun from rising. No other age can compete with the trauma it inflicts upon the human heart. Imagine what wonders await us in the next ten years, the next fifty, the next hundred. Imagine never knowing what these are. Each new discovery opens hundreds of doors to possibilities we've only ever dreamt of. Almost daily the mysteries of life are unravelling before us. We're learning more, understanding more, and thus, we'll miss out on more when we go to the great beyond. Is it any wonder no-one wants to leave? For me there is only one remaining question: what will happen after 25 December 2036? I'd give the world to find out.

---

1.   The other unsettling aspect about the whole saga was being told I'd go belly up on Christmas Day. That's going to make a hole in anyone's

holiday. To think: after a lifetime of moderate struggle, to be remembered as the selfish old goat who ruined the family Christmas of 2036 . . .

Holiday Hell

At every turn a fresh terror awaits. It's all merely part of the escalating stupidity of the silly season. Tiny tears are appearing in the fabric of life. Individually they are nothing, but when they are combined they may rip our world apart. With this in mind I present three inconsequential tirades about things that do not matter.[1]

Cinema Policy

Some Sydney cinemas have adopted a new policy. The poor ushers (they must be rushed off their feet standing there, tearing tickets) have now been given another thankless task by the dim-sighted gang-paranoid management. They're to patrol the aisles of the cinema three times during every screening. Almost overnight these pawns in a much larger game have become the warders of entertainment. Their tour of duty takes them along the aisles and in front of the screen. They're in search of those who transgress the one great law of the cinema: no feet on the seats. All the other laws are mere bylaws: no speaking during the film, no mobile phones, twice the price of admission on the overpriced perishables at the so called 'candy bar'. Surely it would show greater foresight to design a cinema where those who need to relax could put their feet up. For countless centuries now people have been taking this liberty in cinemas. These picture palaces are nothing more than safe houses for the slovenly. Many feel that education, specifically focused on the negative aspects of slouching, is the way to stop this pandemic. It's my belief it will happen regardless, and the best cure is tolerance and acceptance. Besides it's almost certain that once this was allowed it would lose its allure.

There is an immense feeling of betrayal when an usher makes their presence felt. Ours appeared when the world was being destroyed and his annoyingly coiffured head became part of a greater tragedy: a silhouette engulfed in a blaze of friendly fire. These pathetic minions of the dark forces of film deprive us of the basic joys of cinema (which I have deemed fit to list):

1. sitting in the all-enveloping dark
2. drifting away on the dank perfume of stale popcorn and Pepsi permeating the carpet
3. watching the screen
4. (and of utmost importance) being the *spectator*.

Surely when the watcher becomes the watched, and the spectator becomes the spectacle, it destroys the very nature of the medium.

Department Store Policy

Why are there never any sales before Christmas? All the major department stores join in the frenzy of Christmas with ecumenical zeal but they never offer anything in the way of a real gift. Their catalogues are filled with the overt signature of the silly season: red, green, reindeer, snowflakes. But we must be aware that papier-mâché ice castles and Santa are just there to lure innocence, and innocents' guardians, to their fiscal doom. It'd be more convincing if the charity-loving stores of the world, which claim they want nothing more than to bring the *joy of giving* to the masses, marked everything down sometime mid-December. There is nothing more unjust than discovering the financially painful pre-Christmas purchase, now lying broken and discarded in the top room, is a bargain come the start of January. When you witness that poor purchase bundled up with a thousand other loser gifts, when you see it stretched out on the Flanders Field of commerce, when it lies significantly reduced under the red flag of the all-conquering store – it's too much even for the meanest heart.

Big Business Policy

The banks, and big business across the globe, have spent billions ensuring they'll not fall victim to Y2K data-corruption. We've all heard the message, 'Your money is safe.' In the last few post-imaginary-holocaust weeks there's been another development. The ones who must beware the bug's bite are small business and home computer users – the unprepared masses. It's we who'll fall before the monster the commercial empires have brought to heel. Now ask yourself why this makes perfect sense. When there's a discrepancy, as surely there must be, who'll be at fault? The banks who have safeguarded their systems with countless billions from overinflated interest rates and criminal bank fees or Mr and Mrs Nobody? The answer is obvious. This may prove to be the most cunningly devised global conspiracy ever – years in the making – to skim a few more dollars from the deserving poor. Damn Clever.

———

After this work of holiday whimsy I'll leave you with this thought: sometimes you kill crickets thinking they're cockroaches. The time has come to tread carefully.

---

1. The policies listed in this article became standard practice in the final year of the 20th century. Viewed in isolation they are a trifle. However, as an indicator of accepted business practice they create a grim picture of a possible future.

The Celebration of Easter

A long time ago I stayed with a friend from school over the Easter weekend. His parents were ferret-faced university lecturers. Rallying against the commercialisation of Easter they hatched a unique plan. They sent four children into the yard without having hidden a single egg. We entered the garden full of hope at 11 a.m. It was 6 p.m. before the flyscreen door opened again and we were allowed back in the house, our bodies and clothes stained, our anguished faces streaked with tears. His parents smiled and asked us what we had found. We held open our empty hands. They embraced us and said, 'You don't always find what you're looking for.' Then they added, 'You'll never forget this Easter.' And the strange thing is, I never did.

It was a lesson in life that made me obsessed with the true meaning of Easter: the egg hunt. Where no quarter was given and none taken. Where cheating by peeping out a window was mandatory. In the egg hunt there were always winners and losers. Here was a game containing such power it was almost pagan. I would've dragged my arse along a razor-wire fence if there had been an egg waiting for me at the end of it. Sharing the booty was frowned upon. What you found, you had to consume. You became hunter, gatherer, eater: an unholy union of base appetites.

In the pitch of the hunt nothing was beyond the realms of reason. Even though we knew our parents would never place eggs anywhere that put us in peril we checked every possibility. We would blindly stick our hands into stacks of ceramic pots knowing they housed a family of redbacks. We would crawl out on the branch of the old gum knowing it was dangerously close to frayed electrical wires. We would check in the neighbour's yard knowing of his shortsightedness and love of antique guns. (He had once shot the cat with a wax bullet, mistaking the pet for a rabbit. If we were holding eggs in the middle of his yard we could easily be mistaken for rabbits as well.)

When you had the prize you could tell how much your parents loved you. In the family it was one thing – they could try and be impartial – but in the schoolyard it was another. The true test came the next day at school, when you described the type of egg (or eggs) you received. You endured an intensive study concerning the nature of the chocolate, whether or not the gift (or gifts) included any other kind of confectionery, the design and style of the packaging, and the consumer code information and approximate price. Standing alone on the handball courts with your pathetic paper train of caged chocolate eggs you realised the sad truth was your parents didn't love you.

The tragedy for me is that, as an adult, I have not managed to rid myself of the thirst for the hunt. This is the reason I have become unpopular at Easter gatherings. I confess I've pushed young children out of the way to get to the letterbox first. I locked an astute child in a cupboard to keep him out of the running. I am the Philby, Burgess and Maclean of the quest: I have pretended to be an adult, helped hide the eggs and then swapped sides and joined the kids.

I am seldom invited to family functions and have discovered the hunt is less intense when you become the hider and seeker and play alone. Last Easter I crawled along a ledge in an apartment block five storeys above the ground just to get to an egg that *I* had placed there.

My saving grace is that I am not a hoarder. The hoarder is an evil child. Months after Easter the hoarder will still proudly display their stash. This child will walk around untouched by the excess of the chocolate frenzy. The days of pain that traditionally follow Easter will not affect them. Their skin will not be covered in oozing pustulant sores and their stomach will not spasm in revulsion at the mere thought of food. As the rest of the family falls into sickness they'll be smug. But fear not, divine justice will descend upon the hoarder. They will finally peel back the foil, usually sometime in September, to find their beautiful brown chocolate has turned a stomach-churning white. The look of horror and disdain that will contort their face will be worth the wait.

Now let us spare a thought for the ones we never found, the ones that never returned. They're still out there – the eggs we never discovered. Thirty went out and only twenty-eight made it home. Tucked away under the blades of the Victa two-stroke, shoved down the side of a compost bin or in the back of an unused tool kit, they're out there somewhere, in every backyard across this nation – the eggs that never came back.

On Any Sunday

E arly autumn. Grey clouds. Rabid dogs dragging their infected hindquarters down a grassy slope with sexual delight. A distinctly unattractive child wailing, her mouth a combination of dribble, spittle, apple chunks and flies. Couples falling like dominoes into each other's arms, their probing tongues discovering the dental flaws of their partners.

There was no doubt in my mind, the day was a misery.

I took a path less travelled, heading up a hill and away from the seething Sunday mass of fornicators, picnickers and fawning parents. I was anxious, troubled, overcome by an unexpected depression. To distract myself from the dark thoughts I picked up a curious-looking stone. It possessed a fine, somewhat gravelly surface. I turned it over and over again in my hand and discovered it had a perfect spine for sliding my thumb along. For the first time on that curious afternoon I felt a measure of comfort. As I repeatedly ran my thumb against the coarse spine the world changed. The enormous clouds hanging low on the horizon took on a pale-pink hue, and the entire sky appeared suffused with light. The cooing couples with their lock-jaw passion disentangled. Dogs, having sprayed their scent on stationary objects and unfortunate infants, paused to witness the end of the day. And well before I reached the summit I decided I had found a special rock – a lucky stone.

High on the hill I leant on a rail overlooking the park and watched people as they swarmed across the ovals. And as my thumb ran along the rock I realised that sometimes it takes the smallest thing to see the bigger picture. That fragment of stone confirmed the validity of that old cliché: we all need a bit of distance from time to time. Distance from each other, distance from the world.[1]

Viewed in close proximity people are repulsive. Even if we focus on the face (excluding all the loathsome exterior of the body proper), what's so attractive? The thirsty pores, the black nasal hairs, the tired eyes, the wax build-up in the ears, the blemishes, the redness, the swelling? The human face in all its natural glory is grotesque.

As I held my lucky stone, and gazed down from the mountain, I realised something. Every step you take away from people makes them more attractive. If you've never tried this yourself, now may be the time. Distance makes the heart grow fonder, even a few feet can help. Around 10 feet away people are still a little offensive. Those unsettling physical characteristics are fairly clear. No, 10 feet is too close to get any real perspective. By 20 feet people have started to lose a bit of definition. They've lost a certain harshness. They've lost that baked-on grit that our sun can produce. They're starting to soften. By 30 feet they've gone all Doris Day, and at a distance of around 50 feet almost everyone is acceptable, even attractive. At 100 feet everyone is beautiful, or at least they exhibit the potential for beauty. Double this figure and something amazing happens. At 200 feet the miracle of sameness occurs.

At this distance physical differences like hair colour, facial features, colour of skin, shape of eyes, number of limbs and the outward expression of their mental state are all lost. Other potentially damaging features are gone as well: race, religion, personality, halitosis, obesity, anorexia, even gender, as we merge into the same sexless smudge. Once we have passed this important point we never look dissimilar again. In fact the opposite it true. Given distance and a certain amount of density we exhibit a unique oneness. Mixed together in this fashion we become a soft, grey mass – a blob of humanity.[2]

I came down from the mountain and merged with the blob. As darkness descended not only were we all the same but we were all moving in the same direction. We were all heading home. My mood had lifted and I saw a multitude of wonder: love-struck couples hand in hand, satiated dogs and an angelic child whose radiant face could be seen once the food and flies had been removed.

Is it naive to suggest the simplest solution to prejudice, xenophobia and hatred is just a little distance? It's something we should all seek, but not at the same time of course, as that would defeat the purpose. Sometimes things are not what they seem. Take my lucky stone: it turned out to be a hunk of cement – a very comfortable and comforting hunk of cement.

---

1. You may have noticed the exceeding difficulty in getting any 'distance from the world'. In terms of the universe even a plane trip skims the surface. Those who've managed to get a bit of distance from the world and have made the trip to the little stone in the sky have remarked that

the earth is too small for such violent conflict, the moon isn't made of cheese and appearances are deceptive.

2. The only negative aspect of the miracle of sameness is that groups of this size, viewed from a distance en masse, may take on a group persona and become a vicious, belligerent mob.

On the Last Time of Our Lives

[1999]

When I glimpsed the cover I was overcome with fear. I never thought a set of numbers could affect me so profoundly. My heart seized in my chest and I felt unsteady on my feet. When the blood began pumping again my first thought was: if they're making diaries, there's no escaping it. The apocalypse is on its way. Do those numbers, arranged in that particular order, spell out doom? Is there something ominous in that configuration? Mass destruction? The end of the world? Even if you don't believe in numerology it's hard to avoid the mystical properties contained in 1-9-9-9.

Is it mere coincidence that when you divide 1999 by three (the trinity, the number of good) the result is a chilling 666?[1] This is the same number assigned to *the beast* in the book of biblical prophecy, Revelation: 'its number is six hundred and sixty-six'. I don't want to cause undue panic in the middle of the silly season but the world is about to end.

If you don't trust my calculations or the Bible there's always Nostradamus, the Koran, Prince, and every psycho on every street corner. They've all testified the world will end before 2000.

Even T.S. Eliot knew it. In the original version of his historic poem 'The Hollow Men', the last lines read something like:

This is the way the world ends,

on January 1st 1999,

not with a bang but with a whimper.

His publisher persuaded him to remove the reference to the year and thus a timeless classic was written.

You must hurry. You have a few days between Christmas and New Year to collect the canned meats and get ready for the apocalypse. Don't throw anything out after the sleazy or solemn celebrations on the 25th, including those terrible gifts you get every year from the same genetic throwback relatives on your partner's side: you may need them. Get extra batteries for the kids' toys, otherwise they'll go crazy in the shelter. Head for higher ground. It may be fires or pestilence but I'm betting it'll be the old favourite flood theme. If you can't make it to higher ground get a really long snorkel.

Even as you read, biblical prophecy is being fulfilled. People have begun to disappear. Have you noticed that several people who have been with us every week of the year are nowhere to be seen?

You hear the same old stories: it's a nonrating period, they're taking a break. But where have Ray and Kerri-Anne gone?[2] It's my belief they, and other world-famous personalities, know what's about to happen. Due to their respected positions in the media (and Kerri-Anne's connection through *Midday* with psychics) they've found out the truth about the future. These stars of Australian television and many more like them are preparing for The Rapture: the time when those chosen by God will disappear before our eyes and be taken off to Heaven. And who more deserving to sit beside our Heavenly Father than Ray and Kerri-Anne? Ray will be able to ask hard-hitting, no-holds-barred questions about transubstantiation and Kerri-Anne can entertain the angels with the macarena.

The only positive aspect about the world ending is it doesn't matter what New Year's Eve promise you make, because no-one will be around to see if you keep it. If you feel the need to make a resolution, lay it on thick. Why stop smoking when you could free the oppressed minorities of the world? Or why stop swearing when someone's got to come up with the grand unification theory of the universe?

Can there be any doubt that it's happening? Over the last year we've seen the signs: crows flying alone, a sky filled with comets (Leonid), dead wrens, getting out of our bed backwards. In Queensland there have been plagues of locusts (although close up they have the appearance of harmless grasshoppers). Strange weather, bizarre natural disasters, poor moral judgement in political leaders, poisonous water, bad meat, the continuation of *Hey, Hey* all point fixedly to the final days.[3]

And if nothing happens, if the human race survives or we live through the horror, would it be possible to exist, with any semblance of joy, without Ray and Kerri-Anne? You may as well tear the sun from the sky or rip the love from our hearts. Sadly I sense that I too am slipping away. I can feel the edging of my body becoming indistinct and frayed, dissolving. I may soon disappear. So please, enjoy your Christmas and the few days of tranquillity before the New Year. Live it up – for the beginning of the end and the beast cometh.

1. To be honest, when you divide 1998 by three you get 666. When you divide 1999 the result is 666.3 recurring. The recurring 3 tends to make the exercise a little less Satanic and terrifying. I did what a researcher would never do – I falsified the results.

2. At the time this article was written the four pillars of Australian television were still intact: Ray Martin, Kerri-Anne Kennerley, *The Midday Show* and *Hey Hey It's Saturday*. It was a tragedy when three of them did not return from the nonratings period.

3. Had *Hey Hey* continued the world as we know it may not have. The two seemed inextricably linked and only one would be able to make the jump into the future. Thus it was with a heavy heart we opened the door to the year 2000 knowing that Daryl, Red and Plucka were forbidden to cross the threshold into the new millennium.

ON ART

In Praise of the Copy

Originality is dead. The need to be unique and progressive should be condemned as a thing of the past, an antiquated mode of pragmatism that's had its day. Creativity creates contempt, art creates envy and all forms of extreme personal expression leave in their wake the flotsam and jetsam of failed lives.

As a growing number of our literary giants and giantesses are accused of plagiarism, as every second song you hear has the melody of a golden oldie, when contemporary films are identical copies of classic movies, we're forced to accept the notion we're running out of the big concepts. For centuries humanity has tirelessly reworked ageless themes, but it's becoming increasingly apparent that our imagination has a finite capacity for original thought.

These days everywhere you look everyone is copying everyone else. This need not be a bad thing. In recent years the quality of the copy has surpassed the original. It's often more accessible and brings with it a multitude of other enviable characteristics. There is no need to maintain this nonsense that a copy is inferior.

A plastic rubber plant has all the appeal of the real thing, paper flowers will never die and watching *Grease* and *Happy Days* was far superior to living through the unmitigated boredom of the fifties. My own understanding and love of the reproduction comes from personal experience.

When I was a child my family possessed a tea towel emblazoned with Leonardo da Vinci's *Mona Lisa*. This everyday domestic rag possessed all the magnificence of the original portrait but unlike the original it was also functional. We were even lucky enough to have a slight ghosting effect due to a printing fault. In our kitchen the *Mona Lisa* was a tangible beauty, not a pompous, leering mystery behind 6 inches of bullet-proof glass. Years later, when I saw the masterpiece, I was unprepared for how truly dull it was. It certainly could not match the personality of our much-loved tea towel. Where were the years of grease and peanut oil that gave her olive skin a jaundiced glow? Where was the triangular scorch mark that removed her left shoulder? And where was the delicate tear that made her appear the victim of failed facial reconstruction? I left the overcrowded Louvre depressed and elated. In every respect the tea towel interpretation of da Vinci's creation, kept safely in a kitchen drawer, was superior.

In regard to the *Mona Lisa*, Duchamp's version (she has a hot arse) surpasses the original, and our tea towel's exceeds that of Duchamp. Art has always been plagued by plagiarism: da Vinci pinched from Giotto, Rembrandt ripped off Mantegna and Picasso stole any idea that wasn't nailed down. Even Paul Cézanne's self-portrait is said to be a copy of an impression of someone else. The act of borrowing is not limited to the art world but occurs from the boardroom to the tearoom, in every field of research and in every area of study. Perhaps the driving force behind any original idea is the hope that it'll be copied.

When we realise the entire world is engaged in this task we must ask: What's so good about originality? We can delude ourselves, but the majority of us were born to copy – it's in the very fabric of our being. Our bodies are constantly replacing tissue and blood and replicating cells. When we reproduce we give birth to tiny versions of ourselves. As we grow and mature we do so by imitating the actions of others. The title we give to this activity is learning, but in actual fact it's just copying. Our entire education system is based on this act and the winner is the one who copies the best. The hypocrisy here is that if we're caught doing what comes naturally we're branded with the stigma of 'cheat'. We must re-evaluate this system because there are not enough unique thinkers to go around. We should remove the stigma, celebrate the copy, and accept that mimicry is the sincerest form of flattery. Let the rest of the world spend money and time searching for original ideas, and when they find them, we'll do what we've always done – we'll rip them off.

We must not feel too negative about these thoughts. After all, they're nothing new. Most of what is written here is taken verbatim from other articles. I have copied, pilfered quotations and stolen entire paragraphs and who cares? After all, as someone who I can't be bothered naming once said, 'If you steal from one author it's plagiarism, if you steal from many it's research.' We should stop this senseless struggle for the new and accept the supremacy of the copy, the hybrid, the reproduction. It's only human to want to reproduce: we are, in the end, just a copy made in the almighty image of someone else.

The Life and Death of

Inanimate Objects

We wrap them carefully, conscious we were once close. We seal them in boxes. We tape down the tops. We know they can never get out, but we secure them inside anyway, creating little coffins of trinkets that are never let go. We fill the boxes with broken toys, old gifts, letters we cannot bear to read, photographs we cannot bear to see. We establish a mausoleum of memory that grows slowly over the years. Hidden beneath stairs, tucked down behind the couch, at the back of the cupboard, are all the things we once loved. In confined containers of memory, laid out like so many exquisite corpses, are the fascinations and playthings of the past. They're the old friends we've locked away, buried beneath the house or starved of oxygen in carefully stored black garbage bags. It's time to set them free. To release our inert hostages, to experience the garage sale of the soul.

Do inanimate objects have a sense of being? Do they have an independent sense of self that exists outside the investments we bestow upon them? Before we discover them are they waiting for us? Is there preordination in the life of inanimate objects?

And is their life slowly worn down at our fingers? By the grease and the muck, by the acid of our touch, do we eventually kill them?

It must be very difficult for them – these inanimate objects that live and die at our whims. They could be anything: from the crappiest piece of mass-produced nothing that was ever coughed up by a multinational to a stick with a nail through it.[1] When they first enter our lives, fresh and new, we're attracted to them, obsessed by them. We devote time to them, carry them every-where or hurry home to see them again. We breathe life into them. We give them purpose. Then one day, without warning, our mood changes. Overnight we've grown bored with that toy, or that piece of jewellery, or that stick with a nail through it, and we need something new, another distraction. As quickly as the object was embraced it's discarded. Some months later we may pick it up again and remember the good times before we consigned it to oblivion in a box. We all know in our hearts that the humane thing to do would be to get rid of it. But in the back of our minds a voice keeps murmuring, 'Who knows when a sixties *Ben-Hur* plastic sword could come in handy, or half a bottle of putrid soap bubbles from Finland, or a commemorative belt buckle from the Munich Olympics.'

How inhumane and callous it is to hold these inanimate objects in the purgatory of our attics? We must give them a chance to live again – to be dumped and discovered by a stranger who'll love them and nurse them back to life. To keep them locked up is as perverse as hanging onto dead skin. If we continue to hold onto the past, we limit our possible futures.

To illustrate this point: There was once a renowned second-hand dealer who acquired fame because he would never sell anything. His store was overflowing with junk. There was so much wonderful rubbish that he was often forced to sit on the street outside the store. It was here he'd perform his often-protracted and bizarre business dealings. You'd encounter the first hurdle if you saw something you liked. You'd have to get it yourself. This often meant digging at the dirty coalface of his shop-front cave until you'd prised your treasure from the shelves. Finally, with the trophy in hand, you'd inquire about the price, only to find that the article was not for sale. I'm sure he had every intention of flogging all his wares when he woke up of a morning. It was just that, when confronted with the reality of the situation, he couldn't bear to be parted from his goods – from the things he loved. I couldn't fathom if he was a guard imprisoning the merchandise or a guardian protecting it from harm. In all the years I visited his store I was never allowed to purchase anything and I never witnessed a single sale. The store became more and more bloated and still nothing was ever removed. He eventually went out of business.

---

1. I held onto my *American motorcycle cop with real siren action* until there was virtually nothing left of it. The dog chewed the head off the motorcycle cop, then the wind-up engine rusted, the real siren action failed, the rear wheel went missing and the headless cop lost his right leg in an experiment to test the blades of a blender. Years later I saw him again looking better than he had in years. He was in a second-hand store, but for some reason the idiot owner wouldn't sell him to me.

The Art of Ethic Cleansing

We are facing a crisis of epic proportions in this great country. There's a sickness in our cities that is becoming a cultural pandemic: council-approved street art. It's our civic duty to maintain the artistic integrity of our cities. The very reason we have art galleries is to keep this sort of stuff off the street. What sort of world are we creating for our children when bad 'art' can flourish anywhere. If it's good enough to be put inside, it should be put inside. It should be protected from the elements and the vandals. If we must endure street sculptures can they be made more practical than glorified seating? Could they be shelter for the homeless? By day a life-size replica of the Trojan horse, by night accommodation for twenty.

Our cities have always been the sites for artistic atrocities. Do you remember when green was an offensive colour? When enormous communal areas were pebble-creted off and trees and shrubs were removed in favour of pile-encouraging concrete seats? Grey was the approved tone, and drab, lifeless city squares sprang up everywhere. These amazingly sterile and inhuman

spaces looked magnificent on the drawing board. Sparse, archi-
tecturally sound monuments to the Bauhaus and so dysfunctional that people avoided them like the plague. In those days
the streets bristled with life mostly because people were trying
to avoid the abrasive nature of council-approved open spaces.[1]

The mood changed and colour became important again,
leading to an infestation of murals. Any innocent building could
fall prey to a bunch of rabid paint-wielding do-gooders. Murals
began to flood the street art market. You couldn't round a corner
without feeling guilty as another two-storey monstrosity accused
you of not caring for the poor or supporting multinationals or
hating gunga or having lost the child within. Why do murals
always have to point the finger? What allows a wall of paint to
have so much self-righteous indignation? As a medium for social
change murals are about as effective as cabaret. Did a painting
of a dove on a wall ever stop a tank?[2] For ten years I was forced
to find unpainted back streets through suburbs to avoid feeling
ashamed as I scurried away from the murals with my bitterness
intact.

These days murals have given way to sculptures, probably
because you can't paint much on thin air. Empty spaces, much
loved for their lack of pretence, are constantly being filled with
council-approved functional sculptures: shards of pastel glass
you can sit on, bronze parodies of business-suited men, mosaic
bins bristling with bright summer colours and maggots. The
intention of these structures is to humanise the emptiness and
beautify the surrounds. Often in terms of beautifying the
surrounds they're as effective as tinsel and Christmas lights
around a toilet seat.

It seems rational that we return to the old ways if we desire to make lasting and exquisite structures and artistic statements on the streets. For instance, the old clock in the town square in Prague was commissioned by the council of its day and yet it's the most serene and wondrously beautiful creation. It's also one of a kind because when the work was finished the council took a drastic measure to ensure no other council would build a better town clock. They dragged the designer aside and struck out his eyes. A similar story exists for the Taj Mahal: artisans had their hands lopped off so they could never produce such a splendid vision again. To my way of thinking this is a small price to pay. It would also force the artists involved in fashioning these build-ings/sculptures/murals to really think about the worth of their work. Is this elongated bronze of two turkeys sleeping worth my right hand? Is this charming mosaic of two mauve divers chasing a lime-green starfish worth my eyesight? Is this biomorphic puddle of sepia-toned turn-of-the-century snapshots encased in resin worth my life? If the answer is yes, then throw caution to the wind and create.

---

1. The only thing that can live and thrive in these environments is the skateboard. Yet in another unexpected twist of fate these are often the only things banned in these areas.

2. I have no record of a dove, living or painted, stopping a tank. There is the tale, however, that when German bombs fell on the church that houses Leonardo da Vinci's recently restored *Last Supper* every other wall was damaged or destroyed. The *Last Supper* remained untouched and intact. Proof of God or evidence of man's poor aim? Still it's a very, very good mural.

On Art and Valmont's Defence

I n 1928 the *New York Times* art critic Enrico Raffaele wrote
those now immortal words 'I don't know much about art but
I know what I like.' He wrote them in reference to an exhi-
bition of work by the American Dadaist Bert Lange. The dilemma
for the reader was that Raffaele did know a great deal about art.
He was a poet in the Italian futurist movement, instrumental in
the theoretical development of neo-plasticism and contributed to
and edited *De Stijl*, the seminal Bauhaus periodical. Raffaele did
not want to comprehend the difficult conceptual pieces that
Lange presented. Why should you see a painting in the context
of its time? Why should you seek to understand the social and
economic struggles that surrounded its conception or the bloody
battle that greeted its birth? The most exhaustive understanding
of a work will always be defeated by those inane words. There
is no debate: the personal defeats the profound, the pawn takes
the king, the mouse scares the elephant. The only true test is the
test of time: Bert Lange has faded into obscurity while Raffaele's
words live on. I don't know much, but I do know that.

This phrase has become part of the vernacular and I suggest

we broaden its application. We must cast the net wider if we want to use our ignorance as a virtue. I know nothing about car maintenance, entomology or plumbing, and yet I know what I like. Why should we draw the line with art? How many times have you wanted to assert yourself in a field that you know nothing about? It could be politics, literature or bread making. How simple it would be, before any discussion, to profess your naivety. You could then proceed with confidence because you've already stated that you have no idea what you're talking about. It is the perfect way to foil an argument: no-one would be prepared for such a brazen display of honesty. The finest writers and speakers never let the facts intrude on their tales so why should you? The only crime is being discovered, and for that there is an easy solution: be proud, be vacuous and speak on.

In adopting and modifying Raffaele's phrase we would not be setting a precedent. Common phrases have long been used to avoid responsibility. The most recent, and perhaps the most successful, of these phrases was uttered in the film *Dangerous Liaisons*. It was Valmont's defence, structurally seamless, impossible to confront. 'It's beyond my control.' After that film no-one had any control – the man who made the kebabs, the taxi driver, the cinema attendant – no-one accepted responsibility for anything. But it was the banks and the phone companies that clearly profited from this mentality. Their staff became puppets operated by an unseen and evil force beyond anyone's control. I am positive that one bank issued this sentence as the standard response procedure in dealing with all complaints (although it was always prefaced with 'I'm sorry Sir, but . . .').

The major weakness with Valmont's defence is that it is

often used with a smirk.[1] The toadies, lackeys or minions voicing it, aware they're safe in their mental fortress, feel they can afford to be smug. This, in turn, makes the listener want to visit physical violence upon them by sinking a fist into the soft flesh of their head while insanely screaming, 'Is this beyond your control? Is this beyond your control?'

The strength of this phrase lies in the fact that it is difficult to disprove. There is always a superior who governs your actions – someone or something greater and more powerful. So responsibility is guiltlessly abdicated to the next in line, who does the same, in an ascending domino effect, until you reach the highest earthly authority, who follows suit. You are then forced to arrive at the logical conclusion that God, fate or whatever forces shape the world are in control. And let's face it, God and fate are often difficult to confront about the incorrect payment of a phone bill or lost cheques.

Both these phrases have enormous practical application. They can be used with great effect at the office, at home or at the dinner party. Try them over the course of the day in purely domestic situations and witness first hand how effective they can be. Always begin with, 'I don't know much about . . .' If you ever find you've painted yourself into a corner with your own stupidity, retreat behind the impenetrable wall of, 'It's beyond my control.'

Used in tandem they are an unbeatable combination of dumb and shifty. The sooner we incorporate this terminology into our speech, the sooner we can assert ourselves in situations where we have no power. We may be the last to do so, because as far as I can tell, everybody else already has.

1. It is important to note that if you do use this phrase you should not smirk, smile, chortle or grin. The best look is 'concerned middle distance', and repetition does help.

Concerning Miró

On 25 December 1983, the Catalan artist Joan Miró died. The Australian National Gallery in Canberra has one Miró, and I decided to make the pilgrimage to pay homage and bid farewell. The gallery was closed on Christmas Day but on Boxing Day I found myself there. I knew exactly where the Miró was hung. I could have found it blindfolded: left at the entrance, through the Primitive collection, a sharp right at the Tucker just past the shadow of Duchamp's chair and there it was. It owned a vast grey slab of concrete and seemed to vibrate off the wall. I recognised the two biomorphic shapes that were strangely related yet separated by a purple sky and a brilliant red earth. I knew where it had been bumped in transit and a flake of paint had been lost. I sat on one of the black leather couches, sank into the red earth and thought about Miró.

Living in incredible poverty, Miró began suffering hallucinations from lack of food. These intense hallucinations featured the shapes and forms that would become the trademark of his work, simultaneously mature and childlike, profound and simple. Miró understood their potential and sought to summon them from his subconscious. He deprived himself of food and drink and stared at a white wall until figures and surreal creatures materialised before him. These he would scribble onto canvas or scraps of paper. He would capture them in that moment: recording their numerous tendrils, or their misshapen heads, their bloated feet or questing eyes. He trapped the circles, the light, the colours his mind threw up. Beautiful monsters evolved as his white wall turned into a luminous sky, a landscape of dreams.

Miró believed his visions were part of a universal subconscious – the same belief that Jung subscribed to of a common visual language that connects, and exists in, every human being. Miró suspected the reason we were unable to understand these images was that we 'grew up'. He believed that society, education, civilisation and experience all formed a barrier to the intuitive, to the natural, and that everything we learnt prevented us from reaching what we already knew. Miró believed his works were childlike and had to be seen through a child's eyes.

It was with these thoughts falling through my head that I sat and watched the Miró, and a day after his death this is what occurred.

I had been there about twenty minutes when a mother and daughter blocked my view, standing between me and the painting. The little girl was about five and had dragged her mother away from some other pieces to gaze at the bright canvas. She stood twisting her head from one side to another, before her mother asked if she liked the work. The daughter nodded and the mother wanted to know if her little girl knew what the picture was about. She looked puzzled by the question and so her mother began to explain as best she could.

'That's Bugs Bunny and he's under the ocean, and that other ball thing in the water, that's a balloon. You see Bugs has the balloon on a string and he's going over to his good friend Goofy's house . . .'

The mother's astute reading of the work astounded me. Each new observation was a torpedo of bilious popular culture straight into her child's imagination. How was she going to explain *Blue Poles*: 'That's Mickey after his stomach ruptured from too much gentian violet.'?

I was saddened she couldn't create her own myths but had to rely on American cartoons. (I also found it unforgivable that she married a Disney and a Warner Brothers character, something even the most naive child knows would never happen. Goofy and the rabbit were mortal enemies, not to mention the corporations that gave them life.) How could this happen on the day after Miró's death? I felt the artist's dreams had died with him, and it had taken less than twenty-four hours. The description left me desolate.

The little girl continued to twist her head and spoke, quietly at first but gaining in strength and confidence. 'No, it's not. That is the moon and that is a duck.'[2]

In that moment the girl realised Miró's vision. She understood intuitively what her mother could not. Imagination triumphed over reason. It was Boxing Day and I had just received the finest Christmas present from a little girl I would never know.

---

1.   I wanted to do a bit of research on the life of Miró and his work but unfortunately I didn't have the time. However, as a leading political

journalist once told me, 'Never let the facts get in the way of a good story.'

2.   I had thought the name of the painting was *The Moon and the Duck* so I rang the gallery to confirm it. I needed to know that time and emotion hadn't distorted my memory. I discovered, tragically, they had. The gallery said it didn't matter how loud I shouted or how much I swore, it didn't change the fact that it wasn't called what I wanted it to be called. They informed me the painting had the name *Landscape* (*Paysage*) and had always been called *Landscape*. There was, however, one ray of light: the childlike operator who was helping me did refer to the painting more than once as 'that one with the moon and the duck in it'.

CONCERNING TECHNOLOGY

A Critical Mass of
Information

As the heaving beast of technology drags its marketable carcass into the new millennium there is one statement we can make with absolute certainty – the Internet is responsible for all crime in the late 20th century.

It may at first seem grandiose, even preposterous, to make such a claim; however, extensive research and hearsay support this notion. Thousands of eye-witness accounts chronicle the abuse of the information superhighway. These accounts are often from teachers and High Court judges, the most trusted members of our community – many of whom have done years of painstaking research into the Net's more perverse activities. They realise, as we must, this new technology is being corrupted for personal gain. Credit card fraud, get-rich-quick schemes, investment scams, virtual casinos. And our children are learning to make bombs. Bombs more complex and damaging than the ones we used to make. What gives them the right? Where will it all end?

Every article in the paper seems to be accompanied by the

phrase 'from information taken from the Internet'. Or 'a criminal mind inspired by the Internet'. Or 'before the triple murder they met via the Internet'. From children's hobbies to small crimes to government-toppling conspiracies, the Internet is always there. Where did the information about the travel rorts come from? Where do you think! It is time this new toy of the masses stood trial.

We must judge and pass sentence on cyberspace. For too long we have allowed technology to rule our lives and untameable progress to propel us through the years. Each and every technological advancement has been touted as an aid to communication, yet these advancements quickly become symbols of our failure to communicate. Around every home they are scattered like electronic corpses: the television is a life support for the fatigued, the radio thrives on nostalgia and rancid talkback, the telephone is constantly cradled in the iron lung of the answering machine and the mobile phone has become a digital albatross. We can trace it back – the telegraph, the telegram, the Gutenberg press, language. Like papyrus and stone tablets, the Internet is poised to tear apart the moral fabric of our society. Let us not delude ourselves: we cannot control it.

A casual trawl of the Internet reveals many disturbing trends. Adolescent humour, pop groups, conspiracy theories, meerkats, nuclear weaponry, and behind the fluffy facade is the ever-present spectre of pornography.[1]

When I was a child pornography was only available through the careful examination of building sites. Or when it was discovered accidentally, behind a locked door, at the back of a wardrobe, under a pile of clothes in an antique safe, hidden in the deep, dark bowels of the parents' room. Now anyone with half a mind can get their perverted jollies off by a 'quick cruise' of the Net. I wanted to prove this with a grotesque image of obscene proportions taken from my computer. After seventeen hours of searching I still have nothing to download.

Within its Borges-like labyrinth tasteless humour abounds. Imagine what could be achieved if the millions of minds that typed in Diana and Dodi gags were used for good. Imagine if those millions of minds wrote something nice. Something really nice. Something akin to a literary warm fuzzy. A few gentle lines that would enrich humanity, not the vicious puns about Di dying in the smirking Merc. This sort of material degrades us all and only produces the forced laughter of embarrassment or shame. Yes, you may have a private giggle hours later, but this is merely a release of tension that sub-consciously confirms an awareness of your own mortality. Try not to feel too guilty about it.

Too much information is not a good thing. We only have to look at the Library of Alexandria – an ancient equivalent of the Net. Overflowing with plays, novels and epic poems, it was a repository for centuries of Western thought. In the 3rd century it was razed to the ground by well-meaning Christians who despised its liberal Greek texts – the collected knowledge of the world destroyed by fire.

What would the world be like if the library had survived? We would have a plethora of texts comparable to Shakespeare's finest. We would be forced to live in a state of perpetual anxiety – there would be too much choice. Should Year 12 study *The Tempest* or the middle comedies of Antiphanes? Amateur dramatic societies would be thrown into a tizz, choosing between not only Shakespeare and Marlowe but also the lesser works of Aeschylus and Sophocles. In the end it's just more words to read, and if you've read one 'son kills father marries mother gods are angry' epic you've read them all.

Let's face it, it is time for another big fire. Thank God that in the intervening seventeen centuries those well-meaning Christians have kept the torch alight. Not the same Christians, of course, although He does move in mysterious ways.

It is possible to reach critical mass with information. A place where fact and fiction become confused and true meaning is lost. That would be the greatest crime of all.

I cannot recall who said it but it may have been Nero playing the zither at the fire of Carthage: 'Burn, baby, burn.'

---

1. Prior to the Net, porn was sent in brown paper bags through the mail. This means the very same post office that carried our Christmas and engagement cards also carried filth. For years I was a lone voice crying in the wilderness for the closure of this corrupt empire. Others said the mail must get through but I asked, 'At what price?'

The Hole Truth

There is nothing to write about. I have sat in a daze staring blankly into the empty yet luminous screen on my computer. The new file I have created for this task needs to be filled. I have to give it form and substance, to allow it to exist, otherwise it will be condemned to the electronic waste bin. In the days of longhand to take pen to paper was a joy. To mark the feint-ruled virgin white of the sheet with an indelible blue-black ink was powerful, invigorating. To witness a waste bin filled with failure at least gave you a sense of progress. Here there is only the empty flickering screen, the faint hum of the hard drive and the slow clatter of the keyboard. It's difficult to think in this post-Saturday-night state. The contents of my skull are dehydrated, the synapses misfiring, the thoughts muddled. I'm trapped and require something to prise me loose. At present the file and I are one: we're both empty vessels that need to be filled.

Thus, in my less-than-human, slightly nauseated condition, I find myself fixated on a little hole. It's the one thing that has always confused me about my brand of computer. It's an opening on the hard drive just beneath where you place the floppy disk, and if the disk is seized you penetrate the hole with a paper clip to free it. Does this strike anyone else as odd? Surely it's one of the more disturbing aspects of the computer age that if a machine this complex malfunctions it requires a paper clip to fix it. Doesn't this cut against the mythical promise and the entire ethos of the computer age: that we could save forests and jungles from devastation by dispensing with paper? And if we don't have any paper why the hell would we need paper clips? Would we keep them on our desks as a memento of the old days, like reusable plastic Post-its or digital desk calendars?

It's a strange dilemma. You could have an entire library stuck on a floppy but unless you could find a paper clip you wouldn't be able to get it out. The greatest power for centuries at your fingertips, to unlock the stuff of dreams or a second-rate computer game, and it's reliant on a bent strip of metal.

Was it someone's idea of a joke? Why didn't the designers or engineers put an extra little button there, so if something did get stuck, you could simply press it? And why do the disks get stuck in the first place? Couldn't these same designers have designed their computer a bit better so that disks never got stuck? This minuscule advance would take away the need for the paper clip. It might mean a bit more sweat at the drawing board, but someone is paying a fortune to hordes of gifted, bespectacled, sexless freaks for this sort of leap of the imagination. And though I do not want to dwell on the financial outlay, it seems a bit ripe, after you've spent your life savings on this modern marvel of circuitry and science, to have to go out and purchase a paper clip. Is there some government body guarding consumers against this sort of racket? With every computer purchased for over $5000 you should be entitled to a free paper clip. Is that too much to ask? Perhaps my computer manufacturer is in league with paper-clip multinationals? The paper-clip manufacturers, realising their imminent demise, attempted to ensure their survival by crawling into bed with the enemy. Does it come as a surprise the initials of paper clip are PC?

All this may seem like an overreaction, but believe me, when it's late, past the deadline, and the floppy gets stuck, you'll reach for anything to shove in that hole. You tend to lose all sense of reason and propriety. You're driven by the toaster mentality, which dictates that even though you are fully conscious of the dangers involved, when the toast gets stuck you reach instinctively for a knife.

I love my old computer but some days I find myself staring at that little hole and just wondering why. This paper-clip conspiracy may be part of the same oversight that gave birth to the Y2K bug and the potential end of civilisation, but I choose to believe it's a marvellously intricate idea. It raises questions about our overreliance on machines, and at the same time speaks about the interconnectedness of all things. My computer company may have brilliantly presented us with the physical representation of a parable: the lion (computer) needed the mouse (paper clip) to remove the thorn (floppy disc) from its paw (hard drive). What lessons can we learn? The hole has been filled, the screen is full of words and all that remains is to get it out of the machine and down on paper.

The New Horror of

Mobile Phones

We are only too aware of the dangers of mobile phones. Every week there's a new revelation, another test, some more results from a respected laboratory in Sweden that confirms what we all know – that the ultimate evil in society is an ever-shrinking movable means of communication. We know for a fact that it may (or may not) cause brain tumours, glaucoma and debilitating constipation. We have irrefutable evidence of exasperation, frustration and occasional envy. We know that when we get that one call, the call we have waited our whole lives for, the signal will drop out. We have heard the stories of cartloads of mutated rodents sacrificed on the altar of research, we've witnessed the desperate campaigns of terror used to sell these devices, and we've heard of loving families destroyed by outrageous bills. There's already been so much written about the effects of the mobile I am loath to add to the swollen dungheap of hyperbole, conjecture and speculation. But there is a hitherto unexplored phenomenon connected to the mobile phone, an insidious side effect that has not been properly recorded. It is this: it has allowed emotions, once contained or invisible, out into the open.

People can be seen on any street corner pouring themselves and their intense untamed feelings into these dark plastic rectangles. The only thing that separates them from the inco-herent banter of those poor souls who are certifiably insane is the assumption that someone is listening. If the mentally unstable carried mobile phones no-one would look twice. You could be smeared with chicken giblets and carrying a chilled flagon of meth, but if you're speaking into a mobile you're considered completely sane.

Like the woman I witnessed the other day who decided to squat in the middle of a busy pedestrian thoroughfare because she received a call. She gesticulated wildly, laughing like a creature possessed, and had it not been for the phone she would have been carted away. Or the construction worker who blew wet kisses into the phone and spoke to his 'frothy, huggy, lovey dove bear' as he pushed to the front of the queue. Or the businessman who screamed blue murder and abuse into his Vodafone as a group of preschool kids went on an instant journey into the heart of darkness.

When we see these incidents we only witness the effect, not the cause. We see and hear people speaking to the void. The full range of emotions is employed but we only understand half the story. Gone is the balancing image of two or more people relating physically. What we have is one person crying, swearing, singing or smugly flirting with the emptiness. It is the ultimate nihilism.

This aberrant, antisocial and offensive behaviour we're seeing with the mobile is being accepted as normal. And there is a fear that it's spreading. Once, to use a phone on the street, you were encased in a booth. The metal and glass or moulded plastic served to distance and protect you from public scrutiny. You could bang on the glass in frustration, weep into the receiver or sing of universal happiness with relative safety. The mobile has no such barriers. You're vulnerable and connected to a disembodied voice, an electrical spectre, through space (and with a long-distance call, through time as well). You become displaced because the mobile has reduced your awareness of your surroundings and you begin to reveal your true self. And, as anyone knows, the reason we hide our true selves is that we are essentially repulsive. The phone call has forced naked emotion, raw and natural, out on the streets. And raw and natural emotion is, more often than not, fairly ugly. The paradox is that this marvel of technology strips you of the artifice of civilisation.

Over centuries we have managed to house our emotions, shielding them from prying eyes in workplaces and homes. We've confined the beautiful and the brutal – but at the end of the century it's seeping out. Who knows what joys or horrors this will bring? Who dares guess at the world we're creating? If you've the misfortune to find yourself out there on the streets, take a look at the madness we've accepted as rational. The mobile has become as common and as necessary to modern survival as the wristwatch. It makes an appearance at every social and business gathering. It's the natural enemy of the cinema. And although there are attempts to silence its plaintive electronic cry it's always there waiting for the perfect moment to strike. Is there some way to make the mobile less mobile? Can we take away its essential nature, capture and enclose it? Can it come with its own protective booth? Or better still, be chained to a fixed point in the home? At the end of all the research we may discover that the mobile phone has changed our behaviour more than it's corrupted our brain tissue.[1]

---

1. All this being said, it's rude to listen to other people's conversations just as it's considered impolite to stare at them while they weep openly in public. On the other hand, it's becoming acceptable to employ a moderate amount of aggression and vulgarity if the mobile goes off during a film.

The Binding Nature of

Accidents

1967. A half-finished stone wheel is found in the Lascaux cave north of Paris. It's an interesting artefact because it has minute traces of dried blood on its surface. Under forensic examination it's discovered the blood is human. Was this wheel some crude weapon? Was it used in some barbaric rite of passage 40 000 years ago? The patterning and distribution of the blood indicate that it was spilt while making the tool. The only conclusion that can be reached is that it was an unfinished stone wheel made by one of our more clumsy forebears.

To this day most accidents occur in the home. A recent survey has suggested that a staggering 87 per cent of injuries happen in the safety of our domiciles. It doesn't matter if it's the single-storey brick-veneer weatherboard, an adobe hut, an igloo or a million-dollar mansion on the shore of Malibu, people trip over and knock their heads in all of them.

The home lulls us into a false sense of security and this is when fate strikes. It's my belief (although more research is desperately needed in this area) that most of these accidents in the home occur in front of the TV. We take eating and ironing in front of the telly for granted, and yet both are fraught with danger.[1] Other activities I would suggest you be wary of while watching the box: wood turning, drilling, using semi-hallucinogenic wood glues in unventilated space repairing sea-going vessels.

There are ways we can avoid accidents in the home.

1. Stay at work longer.
2. Stay away from your home longer.
3. Live in a hostile, cheerless flat and never get comfortable enough to call it a home.

If there is nothing we can do about the quantity of accidents in the home then we should relocate our homes to be close to medical centres. Some people are fortunate enough to live right next door to hospitals. So when they do have an accident in the home they can just walk across the road (unless, of course the accident in some way limits the use of their legs).

When these attempts fail, we must attempt to make the home a safer environment or move next door to a hospital. On a subconscious level our fear of the home is the reason we go out. Our fear fuels the economy. We huddle together in coffee shops, pour into sports stadiums, enjoy entertainment, concerts, films and linger in the lobbies of casinos purely because we're too terrified to go home. Who in their right mind would stay in their hazardous house when they know outside the front door lies the safety of the streets? It is something our homeless are only too aware of. According to a recent government circular, the homeless aren't homeless for any socioeconomic reasons. They're often just too scared to go home. These people roaming our streets are merely neurotic. They're overcome by the fear of going home to await the inevitable calamity. Another recent survey has shown that nomadic people seldom if ever have accidents. This may be caused by the fact that they are always on the move and thus do not have a place that they could call home. It may also be that because they're never home they never get a chance to fill out any surveys.

As for myself, I have gone several weeks without any domestic mishaps and instead of filling me with a sense of achievement it is having the opposite effect. I realise it's only a matter of time before something hideous comes to pass. Only a matter of time before the oven attacks me, a box drops on my head or the toaster makes a grab for my soul. Each step across the threshold brings with it a sense of foreboding and dread. It has led me to these conclusions: we must broaden the accident base and try and get some accidents out there in the open, on the streets, in the workplaces. Why should our homes have to bear the brunt and cope with the emotional turmoil of being known as the heart of mishaps?

It's the one thing that binds humanity together regardless of race, creed or colour – we're all accident-prone. Across this wondrous earth the only aspect of our nature that truly binds us together is our clumsiness. Forget music, philosophy, and that constant talk of world peace. The only fact that we can be sure of as we stumble and fall into the new century is that we as a people are incompetent. Although we have progressed in almost every other facet of our beings we're still as clumsy and awkward as the Neanderthals who cut their fingers open on shards of stone in the safety of their caves as they tried to make a wheel.

1. To illustrate the horrors of ironing in front of the telly: a gentlemen in Dubbo was engaged in this task when the phone rang. He answered the iron rather than the phone and managed to steam-press his ear.

On Hold

The tree of life, a treasure to behold, sucking carbon from the air and bringing us life-giving oxygen. The tree has long held a sacred place in the mythology and science of humankind. But the image of the tree has been tarnished for me since the advent of phone trees. They have taken root in our communication systems and they're impossible to weed out. I do not believe I am going too far when I say that phone trees are the ultimate evil.

If you want to confirm your tickets, press 1.

What do I press to speak to a human? I want to hear a human voice. Of course, when I speak to a human being I want the machine back.

If you want information about other arrangements, press 2.

Can these people speak any slower? You can be on the phone for 30 minutes and still be talking to the tree. How on earth does that make things quicker?

If timed local calls ever happen in this country, within hours we'll have the economy of Albania. And never get stuck on a phone tree with your mobile. That's the fast track to poverty. You may as well burn your money, at least it'd keep you warm.

I was recently trying to book some tickets for a small trip overseas. Sixteen hours of sheer hell – not the trip, the phone calls. The time I spent on the phone I could have travelled to America, and come back. I was so frustrated and tense I needed a holiday just to get the memory of the phone calls out of my system.

I'll be with you in a minute, Sir.

When did the meaning of the word 'minute' change? Surely a minute is still composed of 60 seconds. These seconds follow each other, one after another, in quick succession, with no significant gaps. Or has the term 'minute' a different meaning when you're on the phone? Is that a 'real minute' or a 'phone minute'. If you're on a phone minute the seasons change, the years come and go, your children grow up and move out. The numerology of the phone minute is fascinating. The phone minute (60) has a function similar to the numerals 40 and 7. It can be used to denote any length of time, e.g. God created the world in a *phone minute*.

As I was passed from one person to another I began to realise I was in a hopeless situation, shuffled from one department to another like a human shuttlecock. Most of the time I was alone in Hold World – limbo for the living. It was there a comforting recorded voice told me what a great service I was getting. That voice always so gosh-darn happy, so infuriatingly understanding, offering me wonderful incentives and letting me know what a clever chap I was for choosing this business.

Spaced evenly between the incentives were the apologies.

Your call is important to us . . . If it's so important, speak to me.

All our operators are busy . . . So employ some more.

We'll be with you shortly ... LIAR! (Will that be in a minute?)

Thank you for calling. And now some music specially designed by the Stasi to torture your brain ... Is it a coincidence that the most offensive tunes humanity has to offer are played every time you're on hold?

My ears suffered the indignity of Roxette as I waited for my six-digit code: I *for Inefficient*, M *for Mistake*, W *for Wait*, L *for Long Wait*, E *for Extra Long Wait*, P *for Pay us NOW*. The six-digit code makes everything more efficient – things really move once those magic numbers are quoted. But to quote them you have to get back on the ol' branches of the phone tree, spend time in Hold World, and speak to Mr I-don't-really-care-if-you-live-or-die Recorded Voice.

Finally I discovered the person I had a problem with was the person I complained to if I had a problem. So I told her I felt something wasn't quite right, she said there was nothing wrong and that's about where it ended. Thank God Kafka never lived to see this.

After the ordeal I had to speak to someone, I had to get it all off my chest. I made the mistake of calling a busy friend. Have you ever tried to tell a deeply personal and traumatic story to someone who has 'call waiting'? It's embarrassingly cruel. It suggests there's someone more important than you, they just haven't called yet, and then there's that tell-tale buzz. Your host expresses their concern and promises to get rid of the annoying caller. You nervously wait for their return, while they see who the other person is. When they come back you know instantly how important you are to them. If they continue the conversation with you it's all okay. (Although if you're a caring person you worry about the caller who's been rejected.) If they say sorry they have another call, you don't mind do you, we'll talk later, this is important . . . you're wretched. You're less important to them than someone you don't know on the other line.

So I'm going to have a holiday – I think I need one – but please, don't expect a phone call.

Tracing a Map of
the Laptop

I am in the back of a taxi hurtling through unfamiliar streets. I have my laptop computer open and I am trying to type out a tale about the influence of movement on writing. Unfortunately, due to the proximity of a reversing truck and the jarring motion of the cab, I have become unsettled. Add to that the faint odour of vomit (unmasked by copious applications of lemon-scented freshness) and you have the perfect ingredients for motion sickness. I have decided to close down the computer before I bring up my breakfast on the active matrix. It would be impossible to remove the stench from the keyboard. But as I have learnt, this is the price you pay when you embark on an experiment in writing.

It's a crime against the laptop to allow it to languish in one spot. To tether it to a wall and make it immobile is against its very nature. The laptop lives to move: it thrives in open spaces and is only ever truly happy when it's out in public. However, although these environments are perfect for the laptop, they may be less than perfect for us. People tend to function at their optimum level when they are in places that are familiar and unmoving. For instance, something written in the stillness of the home has a different feel from something written in a car or aboard an aeroplane or on the upper deck of wind-tossed ferry.

In this piece I have attempted to write a coherent essay in a variety of transport systems, and in a number of unfamiliar places, to establish the effect on the written word.

What follow are my initial observations.

1. As a passenger in a car it's possible to write in a steady, if occasionally distracted, manner. If you must write in a car, find a long, flat road with little scenery. I wouldn't advise driving and writing at the same time. In fact, I think there's a law against it.
2. The bus was a comfortable, unobtrusive place to write until peak hour and then it became virtually impossible. Luckily I gave up my seat to an elderly woman who was so touched by my actions she allowed me to balance my powerbook on her head.
3. If you are attempting public transport, a train on the city loop is best. It gives consistency and familiarity, and it may tie into the cyclical nature of your story – you begin where you end, you end where you begin.
4. The aeroplane is fine as long as the strangers beside you do not feel inclined to talk. Once they have begun, there is no stopping them. They may even pour out their life story because of fear and a shortage of oxygen. If they do, don't take notes in front of them – write it up in the car on the way home from the airport.
5. The ferry: I'd prefer not to talk about this experience. Suffice to say that it's difficult to get the smell out of the keyboard.

It's also the height of bad manners and considered exceedingly poor form to work on your laptop at the cinema. I only mention this as I once saw a critic review a film on his laptop as it was screening. This two-fingered typist from the local rag hammered away in row H illuminated by the glow of his screen and oblivious to the discomfort around him.[1] Normally even the most arrogant critic will restrict themselves to a pen and unobtrusive notepad. Currently there's no etiquette governing the use of the laptop. I would suggest that it's also unwise to use one if you're in a confessional or on any type of roller-coaster ride. All other environments are decent enough if you can find a way of isolating yourself and being unobtrusive. Even coffee shops can be tolerated if you can cope with the constant murmurs of 'wanker' every time someone passes you.

The only conclusion I managed to reach, after all this self-induced pain, is that it's unnatural to write and travel in any direction at the same time. It's disorienting and disturbing and this is precisely why it should be explored. People have always done what is unnatural and this is the reason we've progressed, while other beasties in the fields have done what comes naturally and, as a consequence, are still in the fields. As we continue to push ourselves beyond our limits it's important to know that the laptop will be there to record it all with its stinking keyboard.

---

1. I was positive this self-glorifying freak was writing a review. The only other explanation is that he had attained his highest ever score on Tetras and would not stop for anything, including a film.

The Perpetual Reinvention of
the Toothbrush

I have been brushing my teeth all my life. Every morning and night I enact this ritual that begins and ends each day.[1] Over this time I have witnessed the evolution of the toothbrush and waited on each new development with bated breath. I can remember when you polished your baby pegs with sandpaper and emery board, your gums bleeding so profusely they stained your teeth crimson, the days when you cleaned your teeth with a toilet brush covered with caustic soda, the days you flossed with razor wire and rinsed with unchlorinated water. Happy days, yes, but those days are gone.

Thankfully, every few months for as far back as I can recall, there has been amazing progress in dental hygiene, particularly regarding the toothbrush. This is the result of countless hours of careful research and not token changes meant to inspire a flagging market. In tandem with these advancements for the brush there have been marvellous changes in the paste as well. Fluoride, calcium, tri-colour gels, glitter, minty flavours, peroxide and baking soda[2] – but it is the toothbrush that continues to impress me with its unceasing transformation.

I believe the toothbrush had to evolve to combat plaque. Plaque spread like an evil communist plague across the free expanse of our teeth. It turned our God-given beaming white molars into decay-ridden grey enamel condos for bacteria. It corrupted, tarnished and ultimately destroyed. We craved freedom from the tyranny of tartar just as we demanded safety from the Soviet hordes. Over the years both desires were met. The new brushes tore down the wall of grey filth as easily as another wall fell in Berlin. We may think we have defeated plaque, but it will never rest, and we must be vigilant in case it ever rears its ugly head again.

You'd think with these continual changes the humble toothbrush would be the most exceptional piece of bathroom hardware, yet it has remained essentially the same. A solid piece of plastic measuring 18–20 cm in length (roughly the distance from the tip of the index finger to the wrist) with a collection of scrubbing bristles at one end. It is in the minute detail that the brush has undergone dramatic modification. The array and choice of the modern brush is a testament to our free society. It means no-one need go unbrushed – regardless of your dental state, there will be something to suit you.

The antiquated and cumbersome rectangular head that ruthlessly tore your gums has been replaced by a streamlined diamond head. If the diamond head fails to satisfy, there's the advanced rounded head or any number of geometric shapes you can stick in your mouth. Angled, tapered, compacted with an articulated neck, this implement (nothing more than a stick with hair) defines the need for design.

Toothbrushes are no longer slippery lumps of four-by-two that fly out of your hand at a moment's notice. These days they have rubber pads for greater control and thumb grips for assured manoeuvrability. Never before has a toothbrush felt so comfortable in the hand or flown so effortlessly over our teeth, never before has it felt so natural in your cakehole.

Then there's the bristles (what a limited word for the modern wonder of these dental excavators). The bristles of today are longer than ever before, enabling them to reach further, push deeper. Why didn't someone think of this earlier? They're rippled for maximum plaque removal, polished with rounded ends to prevent irritation, and recently they have become *micro-textured*. I pity the generations that have passed away never knowing the joy of the indicator brush: a brush that gives you a visual sign it needs to be replaced. No longer do you have to peer at the frayed head wondering whether it's time for a new brush. Now a fading blue line alerts you before you have time for concern. How stupid we were using shabby and worn brushes that were ineffective and perhaps dangerous. With the indicator brush a look at the bristles is all it takes.

Forgive me: for all these extraordinary advances, I can't feel the difference. How can something in a state of constant change look exactly the same? And how much further has the toothbrush got to go? When will the designers and the builders say, 'This is it – the pinnacle of oral hygiene'? I fear the toothbrush of today will be nothing in comparison with the toothbrush of tomorrow. And yet, as long as the toothbrush continues to evolve, we can safely say, 'We live in the free world!'

---

1. Occasionally I have failed in this ritual. The reasons are many and varied although more often than not I have been overcome by

bacchanalian excess and preferred, as I slipped into a comatose slumber, the acidic taste of bile in my mouth.

2. Baking soda. There's a radical concept, a revolutionary breakthrough in the 'fight for white' – baking soda. Just like your great, great dead-as-a-doornail with-no-teeth-left-in-her-head grandmother used to use. And although it isn't discussed, if it can suck up the odours in the fridge imagine what it can do for your halitosis. 'The rest of her body has rotted away but her mouth is still as fresh as the day she died.'

CONCERNING THE TITANIC

The film that defined the excesses of the 20th century was James Cameron's *Titanic*. The impact and impression it left on a stunned populace can still be felt today. In its wake were broken hearts, empty wallets and the distressing knowledge there could never be a sequel.

In all truth this was a disaster movie.

Titanic

• Part 1

[a question of size]

I fought my way to a decent position in the middle of the cinema. (I abandoned long ago sitting at the rear of the picture house where the slurping sounds are somehow more annoying because they're *not* connected with food.) I was early and the sombre warmth of the dark cinema lulled me into a sense of wellbeing. Meanwhile the forces of evil were rallying at the candy counter. Before I knew what was happening the place was awash with people. A group of lanky students invaded my aisle from the left and on the right two large buckets of popcorn sat down. They trapped me in a pincer movement. I consoled myself with the fact there was no-one sitting in front of me, just as someone did. Not just someone – someone who insisted on sitting up straight, someone with good posture. Why is it people with bad posture never sit in front of you? Where are the people who slouch when you need them? No, I get a 7 foot tall basketball-playing pinhead and his little dreadlocked friend.

I recently saw *Titanic*. I do not pretend to be a film critic and so I will not discuss the merits or otherwise of the picture. Given this tragic voyage is so well known I do not believe I am giving away too much by telling you the ship sinks and a great number of people drown. The central theme of the film is the enduring nature of love. The two main characters find that wealth and the trappings of opulence have no hold over this simple joy. I wondered why the most expensive film ever made in the history of humanity had to tell us this? By its mere existence it suggests that perhaps there is something quite beneficial about having a great amount of money. Money and Love, Good vs Evil, Man against Woman, everyone competing against Nature. It's a titanic struggle across the screen between big themes and bigger budgets. Of course I'm concerned with size but it's always the little things that grab my attention.

Why is it big things can be totally overpowered by little things? The big thing I refer to here is the film, the little things are the annoying habits of other human beings. *Titanic* – a massive project, years in the making, costing millions of dollars, employing thousands of workers, and it can all be destroyed by someone sitting in front of you with itchy dreadlocks.

The titles blazed over my head, engulfing me in 72 mm grandeur, and my attention was dragged to this weird guttural noise, like a toad regurgitating its own phlegm – it was coming from the pinhead. How is it one persistent cough can overcome even the most sophisticated audio system? Yes, the audience *is* listening: to the slurping of watered-down post-mix, to the crunching of popcorn and to the clumsy passion of 14-year-olds. This is a monumental undertaking that should totally absorb me in its fantasy and yet I get distracted by Gumby and his mate slowly tearing open a bag of Burger Rings. I tried to incorporate this into the film. I imagined the waiters serving Pommery and Burger Rings to snobbish first-class passengers, their saliva turning the Rings to mush. I was about twenty minutes in when the dreadhead began to rock. He managed to rock rhythmically for over two hours, only pausing to take something out of his bag, and he even managed to do that quite loudly. It was jarring for me that Bullwinkle and Rocky were enjoying the film so much. And why not? They were well fed, they were having good conversations, the little one was even dancing.

It amazed me that all these minuscule, insignificant, puerile and petty things conspired to drag my attention away from the most expensive film ever made. I thought of David and Goliath, the mouse and the elephant, I even managed to relate it back to the iceberg and the *Titanic*. At that moment I came back to the film. I no longer cared if the dreads left a trail of grease over my leg every time Rocky leant back. I didn't care about the moose and his pleurisy. I couldn't care less if he was suffering from TB coughing up great hunks of blood over his Burger Rings. I was aboard *Titanic* and heading out to the open seas on a wonderful adventure.

I focused all my attention on the screen. I broke through. I conquered those annoying little things and could now concentrate on the big picture – a film about water. Lots of it, dripping, gurgling, swishing, trickling, dribbling, pouring in. Something inside me responded to the swirling majesty of the ocean, something deep within me stirred. It was an hour and a half after the film started when my body decided to betray me and I faced the true terror, the true torment of *TITANIC* . . .

Titanic

• Part 2

[the struggle continues ...]

I have thought about it for quite some time and there is no easy way to say it. I have tried euphemisms and analogies, but all these pleasantries do is distract from the importance of the information. It is best in these moments to be brief and blunt, so please, do not be shocked at what I am about to say.

My message is simply this: empty your bladder before you see *Titanic*. Especially the very young or elderly. You may be offended by my brutality now but you will thank me for it later. I made the mistake of seeing the film on a full tank. I thought I had an unburstable bladder of steel. I thought I could defy this film. When it ran for over three hours I was worried. But the duration of the film was not the real problem. The real problem was the water. A digitally enhanced ocean in luminous 72 mm crashing all around me. Every time it lapped against the hull it called to its aquatic doppelgänger, its discoloured sibling resting in my bladder, to come join it.

There is so much water in this film it deserves its own credit. When it's not streaming through shattered cabin doors or bursting through stained glass it's steaming windows, moistening cheeks, disguised as champagne or summoned as spit. Not a scene goes by without some poor relation of H_2O making a guest appearance.

Every time the sea burst a pipe, eddied in a stairwell or careened through the corridors I understood the shallow meaning of water torture. When the captain stood on the deck of his sinking ship and twin jets sprayed in arcs across his chest my bladder cried out in sympathy. It, like the waters of the Atlantic, needed to express its nature.

Even when there was no water in shot I heard it – about to enter like an over-eager actor shuffling his feet outside the door. It burbled, sprinkled, dripped and announced its wetness without being seen. It was always there and it was always calling, calling, calling . . .

And as water forced its way into the body of the *Titanic* it was trying to force its way out of mine.

I thought to myself: I'll be damned if I let this rebel organ dictate my actions. Why should I let one part of my body defeat all the others? If I leave I'll lose the plot. I'd made a financial investment in this feature and a little internal pressure was not going to waste my hard-earned cash. I decided to grit my teeth, gird my loins, bear down and stay seated. I was going to brave it out! I crossed my legs, I hunched forward, I loosened my trousers. I settled back and relaxed (but I didn't relax too much).

I then noticed the entire cinema sat cross-legged, hunched forward and slightly distracted. With this awareness my panic dissipated. I felt a connection, a unity with my straining comrades.

Seconds later I was also aware I wouldn't be the only one

heading to the toilet at the end of the film. My new comrades instantly became the enemy and I eyed them with contempt. Images flooded my mind of overcrowded urinals and columns of misery stretching from each cubicle. I saw damp fathers pointing their exploding sons at the trough, rolls of wet toilet paper, and so much acrid spray that the lavatory became a steamroom. Agonised, distressed faces, twisted in hellish torment (many of them from an earlier session).

I lost the battle with the bloat minutes before *Titanic* ended. I rushed out a street exit knowing everyone else would be heading to the foyer. I found myself in a poorly lit, uninhabited back alley. I unleashed the beast and opened the floodgates. I surprised myself with the monstrous torrent issuing from my body. Every muscle sighed with relief; even my mind seemed clearer. Clear enough to realise what I took as a back alley was, in fact, a major pedestrian thoroughfare. Those members of the audience with stronger constitutions than I were now using this handy walkway to get to their cars. Sadly the sight of disgusted families was not enough to stem the tide. They scurried by, shielding the eyes of their children.

I clamped down but I couldn't stop. I was a liquid blimp, a urine geyser, a 4 litre wine cask being squeezed dry by the hand of God – 90 per cent water and 70 per cent of it heading into the gutter. Hours passed, as did half the population of Sydney, before it slowed and finally stopped. I crept off into the night, noticing I was not the only one profoundly affected by the movie. The city was drenched.

The true magic of this epic will not be seen in the streams of people with satisfied faces leaving the cinema but in the streams of people with satisfied faces behind the cinema. I suspect it's going to be a long, wet summer.

One lesson I learnt from *Titanic* is that the little things will always overpower the large – and it doesn't matter if it's a weak bladder or the tip of an iceberg.

Titanic

• Part 3

[the continuing case against ...]

I have always thought that the purpose of entertainment on
planes was to lull you into a soporific dullness in preparation
for sleep. As the meal sets like concrete in your stomach,
and the cabin lights dim, the stewards administer your movie
like a medication – a visual narcotic designed to knock you out.
Before you know it you have become a lesser instrument in the
orchestra of snoring that can at times overpower the roar of the
jet engines.

When an airline shows films it is common sense for it to steer
away from disaster movies. Who needs to create a panic when
you're 20 000 feet up in the air. For this reason alone the *Airport*
series, *Die Harder* and *Death at 20 000 Feet* were never shown,
and you would be hard pressed to see informative documentaries
like *Black Box* on any Airbus. Images of planes exploding or over-
shooting the runway, the sight of passengers consumed by
flaming fireballs or of terrorists holding guns to a pilot's head
are not the best midair fodder. In the relative safety of a cinema
these flights of fancy are fine but they'd be disconcerting aboard
a Boeing, especially if they were jumbled up with glimpses of

reality as you reeled in and out of an unsettled sleep.

All this being considered, it came as a shock to me that the most monumental disaster movie of recent years was the in-flight movie on my recent overseas trip. I am aware the film was touted as the greatest love story of the preceding six months, but there is something a little more to it than that. It is also loosely based on one of the greatest tragedies of the 20th century. It doesn't seem a great jump to me to envisage the Jumbo as the *Titanic*: on the most rudimentary level even the names seem to be linked. It's not a dissimilar situation: a large vessel carrying hundreds of people from different walks of life to a destination half a world away, with a stoic, sexually repressed first class and an economy section dominated by pagan lust and Irish dancing.

The previous film I endured on an international flight was entitled *The Edge*. In the in-flight version of the film a light-aircraft crash, which I would consider pivotal to the plot, was lovingly omitted. When the intrepid explorers, previously sparring in the cabin of the plane, found themselves alive and in water it was left up to the viewer to piece together what had occurred. We were aided slightly by the debris of the aircraft floating around the survivors as they paddled for the shore. Later in the story these same explorers violently fought a grizzly bear, which they allowed us to see. In *The Edge* it is understandable that we might make the connection that we are also in a plane and therefore in danger of falling from the sky, whereas a bear is less likely to wander out of the galley in search of food with the scent of blood scorching its nostrils.

And I assumed with *Titanic*, as in *The Edge*, at the first sight of the iceberg the film would sensibly conclude. We would be spared the horror of the catastrophe, the mayhem, the loss of life and equally the accompanying thoughts of our own mortality. It was not to be. The boat went down. People died. Bodies tumbled through space – skewered, severed and dismembered – or they fell into the freezing water and drowned. Sadly they possessed no life jackets with little whistles and lights to attract attention. We were infinitely better off, but in the case of a disaster weren't we all in the same boat. Even armed with the knowledge that 'in the event of an emergency masks would drop from the ceiling' I could sense a growing disquiet in economy – the only survivors of the *Titanic* disaster were rich. These flimsy curtains would not hold us back from those scoundrels in first class, and had the majority of us not been snoring there could have been a riot. I sat watching my sleeping companions wondering how many I would have to crawl over in order to save myself.

I wondered as I left the flight if *Titanic* was being shown with such abandon on any ocean cruises. You could combine it with the German classic *Das Boot* for a double-header of claustrophobic-watery-hell action. I'm sure they'd tell you, as they rearranged the deck chairs on the *Sea Princess*, it could never happen here.[1]

1.　The other disconcerting aspect about the flight was that asparagus was served to accompany the main meal. On the surface this may not seem much of a problem. However, once this marvellous vegetable is processed by the body it exits with the most acrid odour. I believe aircraft cuisine should never be hampered by the limitations of travel – it should attempt to attain the highest level of the culinary art even if it is served from little plates off a trolley. And while the head chef should let the creative juices run wild they should realise we can't. It hardly seems the height of wisdom to condemn several hundred people, trapped together for twenty-four hours in a confined space, to the violently strong odour of their own bodily functions. The dual dilemma here is that *Titanic* has the ability to force even the most resilient bladder to spill forth and gush like a geyser. The combination of this film and the asparagus was so diabolically evil I prayed it was more than mere chance.

ON POLITICS

God, King and Country

Preface to the Piece

In 1999 the people of Australia were asked to consider the question of our future. The answer we gave surprised the world, baffled the Monarchy and shocked the faithful.

The Piece

Who are we? Where are we going? These are questions of identity that we as individuals hope to answer. They may take a lifetime to sort through. They may baffle us, changing from one year to the next, and the answers may ultimately evade us. Yet these questions are essential. They give us definition and form and they're rarely, if ever, asked by entire nations. This is why the Republic debate is such an important issue.

Should we enter the next century as a Republic, uncertain, with faltering footsteps, yet independent? Or should we stay with the Monarchy – the Monarchy with its familiarity, its rich history of atrocities, intolerance and inbreeding? The decision is a difficult one. I have always been a Monarchist – the high cost of independence is frightening[1] – but a recent dream has caused me to rethink my position.

In the dream I'm a cloud passing over the violent landscape of Gallipoli. Young Australian soldiers are pinned down by Turkish guns. A sour-faced sergeant, little older than the men in his charge, stalks the trench searching for the first wave of volunteers. He knows he's sending the hope of the future on a suicide mission. His powerful words of encouragement cannot disguise his trembling voice: 'Who'll go over the top for God, Howard and Country?' At this point in the dream the soldiers look at each other. They shuffle uneasily on their feet. There is uncertainty in their eyes . . .

Some of us may live in worlds of candy floss and daydreams but those realists among us know that war is an ever-present danger. And in times of war will our brave lads and lassies rally to the call *For God, Howard and Country*. It's stirring, it strikes in your chest, but something about the middle part just doesn't ring true.

There was a time when I would have killed and maimed others for the greater glory of God and for Queen/King and Country. (It began around 1066 and ended with the charge of the Light Brigade. My early education could be at fault here in giving this period of combat a chivalrous feel.) I'd have gleefully committed atrocious acts for my King but in the near future, with Charles in charge, I might have a second thought. And the battlefield is no place for second thoughts. At least that's what I am led to believe, having never been on the battlefield. Could you procrastinate on the field of glory? Before you rode into the Valley of Death could there be time for quiet reflection?

Like the soldiers in my dream I am dubious about going over the top for Howard. It isn't a political thing. I have qualms about 'going over the top' for Beazley and Lees as well. And no-one coming up through the ranks is inspiring me to kill, either.

Faced with this hurdle we could simply reduce the statement to *For God and Country* and leave out the messy uncertain bit. The problem then becomes the belief or non-belief in an omnipotent being who oversees and governs all our actions. Assuming our war to be a just one, we'd be engaged in mortal combat with his other less politically sound creations, who also believe this fickle god is on their side. We live in a multicultural society with a host of different creeds that must be supported by this sweeping statement. What about all those noble Aussies going into battle for Buddha, Krishna, Osiris, Odin, Mars, and a host of lesser-known deities? Will the powerful Satanist lobby, which is always well represented in times of war, be upset by all this talk of God? What about the pagans? Going over the top for Howard, woodland sprites and faeries would be even more embarrassing.

In the end it comes down to *For Country*. Which sounds a trifle brief. The only other avenue available to us is not to go to war, thus avoiding any need to 'go over the top'. We might be able to achieve this in the next century by settling disputes with dialogue and compromise. On the other hand, a new nation needs a baptism of fire. And what better baptism than a damn good war. There's no doubt it's confusing trying to discover your national identity, especially when you have multiple personalities to deal with. So we find ourselves back at the beginning with the same questions to answer: Who are we? Where are we going?

1. One can understand the terrible cost of independence when one sees what has happened to Canada. This once-proud arm of the empire, this beatific British enclave, has been transformed into a barbaric place. Its citizens are forbidden to perform the plays of Shakespeare, they never see fine BBC productions like *Yes, Prime Minister* and they've been forced in some areas to speak French. If we place ourselves in the hands of these in-fighting republican aesthetes, will we suffer a similar fate? Am I alone in saying '*La mort avant le français*'?

The Process of Democracy

It approaches. The fear tactics and scare-mongering campaigns of the opposing parties are in full swing. There is, however, an aspect of this upcoming referendum that's escaped the notice of the general public and has been stealthily avoided by the muck-raking protagonists: the archaic method we employ to cast our vote.

It's a dire state of affairs that in the new millennium we will be forced to acknowledge to our grandchildren that their fate was decided in a cardboard box. Polling day is an overrated and outdated exercise – a day when you're forced to mingle with members of opposing political persuasions, crammed into a claustrophobic cardboard box to assert your democratic rights, with the only hope in sight being the mandatory sausage sizzle. Entering a cardboard booth that has just been vacated by a total stranger cannot be healthy for ourselves or our children. That last voter could have come from anywhere. With our lax judicial system they may even have been a convicted felon. Make no mistake: in this less populous land of the free, many of those other voters are thieves, criminals and murders.

You'd feel safer voting in the country, knowing half the folks that came to vote and being related to the others. The problem with the city is the large diversity of people sardined into a relatively small area. On the day of the referendum, when we're called out to do our patriotic duty, will we be placing ourselves in incredible danger?

Due to the thoughtless design of the cardboard booths, our ballot-casting hips end up jutting into no-man's-land, presenting the perfect prize to the petty crim. While you, noble citizen, are obsessed with the dilemma of our future and momentarily dazed by the YES/NO question, filthy fingers may be primed to pilfer your possessions. Cardboard offers little protection for your valuables or against the vicious thrust of a knife or, indeed, against the sneeze of a passing voter. This is the other great, yet oft ignored, danger of communal voting. How many times have you entered a polling booth to be confronted by an unusual smell, an uncomfortable stickiness, a mess of paper or a mound of dead skin?

After years of voting all I can honestly say is that the following day I felt sick – sick to the stomach and racked with anguish that I had once again failed to divine the populist sentiment and pick a political winner. At least that is what I believed until a moderate amount of research revealed the true cause of my sickness: cardboard boxes are breeding grounds for disease. The last great outbreak of salmonella poisoning in Canada came from a bacteria-laden hot dog on polling day. Let us not forget that the typhoid epidemic of 1872 began in a polling booth. We need only look to our northern neighbours to witness the dangers inherent in voting. Is it worthwhile, even for the sake of liberty, to be exposed to tuberculosis, consumption, numerous venereal diseases and the possibility of theft or death?

Voting must move with the times. We should cease these feeble attempts to make it a community event and home in on comfort. Why leave the security of our homes to cast a vote? We have the Internet, phone lines and the ultimate product of freedom, the TV. If this century has been about anything it has been the struggle for freedom. The humble box has spread the plague of democracy more effectively than any other method. It introduced into the vacuum left by totalitarian states and communist regimes a seductive world of wonder. Who could resist its dizzying array of colours, its distorted view of reality and its seemingly endless, yet almost affordable, products? Thus the best way to comprehend our present notion of freedom is to appreciate that it's directly related to the number of TV stations one can receive. In Australia we're relatively free compared to some developing nations, which are only now fully understanding these concepts, with the help of MTV.[1] In the States they enjoy rubbing their excessive cable-loving freedom in our faces. In this original Land of the Free there's so much high-quality TV that it's hard, if not impossible, to leave the home.

It's my belief that contemporary cultures should vote by remote. (The technical aspect we can leave up to the CSIRO.) Everyone who is anyone has a remote. The only people who don't are the poor, the homeless and those who have rejected the TV as the most culturally significant icon of the late 20th century. These people through their own action, or inaction, should be ineligible to vote anyway. They clearly have no desire to live in the present and should be relegated to the past. It's time to bring the two great traditions of democracy and TV together. It's time to accept the future, to embrace a new nation. In short it's time to vote by remote.

---

1. Tragically, in Australia some country areas have limited freedom due to the placement of transmitters.

Concerning Mandatory

Sentencing

Hopefully by the time you read this the situation will have changed. As it is today, there is nothing else that I can think of. I attempted to divert myself with something inconsequential: something light and suitably Sunday – a midafternoon snack of words that was easy to digest and discard. But my mind continues to return to mandatory sentencing.

'Three strikes and you're out' was the convenient sporty phrase that described a great American initiative. If an offender committed a third crime then regardless of the nature of that crime, or the reasons behind it, they would face a jail term. It was thought this hard-but-fair attitude towards repeat offenders would put an end to their antisocial behaviour and transform them into worthy citizens. The net result was more young villains entering the already overpopulated prison system.

Here in Australia, we mocked the new law in our nightly news and ridiculed it in our papers. We understood that something as backward and transparent could never happen in our country. Our distance gave us a certain objectivity. We agreed that a good Christian people were entitled to protect their property even if it amounted to nothing more than a biscuit, coloured pencils, 40 cents or a tin o' beans. It was, after all, America – the home of the brave, the land of liberty. This response was totally understandable in those states where crime was out of control and watermelon-eating redneck yokels and their white-bread-fed banjo-playing cousins would dance and fornicate all night to white-supremacist rap music blissfully unaware of the irony. (Forgive the generalisation.) It was America and these sorts of discrepancies made sense there. We took the moral high ground secure in the knowledge that our country would never attempt something so shallow. After all, we didn't have the baseball connection that somehow legitimised the notion with its *Forrest Gump* simplicity.

Now, many years later, we have adopted this novel law with devastating consequences. With mandatory sentencing it's a foregone conclusion that you will spend some time in 'the big house'. Why bother with the expense and artifice of a judge? Anyone could gavel you into jail. We could take it in turns. It'd be the gratifying and fun alternative to jury duty. Conscience-free condemnation.

And why merely follow the American system? Why blindly adhere to its out-of-date method of dealing with the criminal element? There is an opportunity here for genuine creativity in law making. Don't give offenders the opportunity to become repeat offenders. Patiently waiting for a second or third violation is appallingly liberal of us. Anyone in their right mind is going to have one or two goes if you're allowed three cracks at crime. If they do it once, they'll do it again: as surely as night follows day, a tiger can't change its spots, and one bad egg can spoil the whole barrel of apples. Let's join together to really shock the international community: one strike, you fry. It saves time, money and paperwork. It's only fair (although that doesn't seem to be a concern).

Given our own history, petty crime is something that should be applauded, so that it can continue to form the backbone of our cultural identity. Over two hundred years ago the foundations of white Australia were laid on petty crime. We may have been riding on the sheep's back but it's a near certainty that the animal was pinched from some undeservingly wealthy landed gentry – some narrow-necked, fine-nosed, high-society type, born with a silver spoon in their arse and a colostomy bag wired to their mouth. Crime has played an integral part in developing our much-lauded larrikin spirit. It has given us our universal identity as a nation of convicts. We were the hard-done-by, the underdogs. Our folklore, our pale songlines, are steeped in tales and tunes of wild colonial boys, charming thieves and mother-loving murderers. Even our most famous ballad, our unofficial national anthem, is about a thief – a wanderer, a vagabond, who stole a jumbuck for food. It's a song that arose out of a sense of injustice, a song we sang to comprehend our place in the world. Our history lessons spoke of an underclass that prevailed against all odds and triumphed in a harsh and alien environment.

And yet, now that our own scars are healed, rather than learning from the wisdom of the ages, we have chosen to inflict the same brutal punishment upon those who we believe are under our power. What sad songs will we write now? And how many more ghosts will waltz before we acknowledge the error of our ways?

ON SCHOOL

Morality and Relaxation

We were told to lie flat on the floor looking up at the ceiling. The carpet was a thin grey-and-blue weave on which hundreds of boys had lain before. I could feel how worn away it was beneath my body. We were told to close our eyes and relax.

The room itself was large and had been painted a distasteful off-yellow. The curtains were drawn and all the lights turned out. Regardless of these measures the sun managed to infiltrate the space. It oozed through the curtains, it permeated the weatherboard, it heated the air making everything seem close and uncomfortable. As a result the room wasn't so much black as a disquieting shade of grey.

Your fingers are becoming numb. The numbness is creeping up your arms. You feel heavy. Your limbs are like lead weights.

His voice floated over our heads and I tried to feel numb but something kept distracting me. It was a short, sharp zap accompanied by the faint odour of death.

Concentrate on your breathing.

There was a record playing. 'In Search of the Lost Chord' by the Moody Blues. Between its obvious drug references and Eastern mysticism I could definitely hear a flute playing. They spoke of Timothy Leary and astral travel. They incorporated 'OM' into their dense lyric structure. They had yantras printed on the gatefold sleeve of the record. I expect you were meant to tune into this mid-sixties groove by smoking a reefer, riding the white dragon or dropping a tab. You know, 'Let your body go loose baby and spin out to the mind-numbing hallucinogenic wonder of the Moodies.' But I think a lot of the deeper connections were lost on 130 adolescent schoolboys lying on their backs.

Where was that noise coming from?

Let the air enter through your mouth, breathe in and let it leave through your nostrils, breathe out.

I found it. My eyes were wide open and fixed on a device hanging off the wall. It was slightly to the left above my head and it was more amazing than anything else that was going on. A perfect halo of shimmering blue in a cage of white wire. A fly zapper, but it didn't seem to discriminate: any creeping, crawling, flying thing was treated in the same manner – instantaneous death.

As the rest of the class commenced their inward journey I was stuck outside myself. I couldn't tear my eyes from it. This thing of luminous beauty seemed to take on a life of its own.

You are in the universe and the universe is in you . . .

The humming machine claimed another victim. It was curious to contemplate my mortality while insects unwittingly discovered theirs. I was trying to sink deeper and deeper into myself to come to a greater understanding of my role in the universe, while the game of life was being enacted right in front of me. I wondered if it would always be that way: life and death, just out of reach, above my head.

Breathe slowly, listen to your heart . . .

But my heart was a dull, distant drum and quite boring alongside the intermittent crackle of the zapper. That sound had spirit and zest. That sound was dynamic. That sound was going places. That was the sound of the eternal struggle. I think someone had started snoring.

You are on a journey . . . Into inner space . . . Into silence . . .

God, that thing was good. There weren't this many bugs in all of Christendom. I was sure some of these tiny beasties were flying from miles away just to see it. 'Yeah man, a beautiful circle of blue. C'mon, let's take a closer look.' Excited moths in other countries dreaming of the day they'd see the light. It never faltered, it never failed, it just kept going and I found the consistency disturbing. Not a minute passed without some poor creature colliding with the infinite. It was tireless, systematic, and it made no moral judgement about the killing. There had to be some heavy karma happening there. A crackle of electricity, a plume of smoke, and the charcoaled body of another moth was fused forever to what it had most desired. The blue neon kept up its merciless crusade.

Imagine a light.

I didn't have to, it was there! A halo luring innocence to its doom. I watched, transfixed by the little sacrifices to the circular blue neon. The quest for inner peace was lost on me. Where the others found their souls illuminated, I saw burnt-out carcasses; where they glimpsed heaven within, I saw fragments of transparent wings.

The Desire for the Old
School Tie

The days spent in school govern the rest of our lives. How many of us huddle round the water cooler at 10.30 a.m. because of some trace memory of 'little lunch'? Or at 2 p.m. start looking at the clock, tortured by the laborious movements of the hands? Or by 3.30 p.m. need to sink into a lime-green vinyl beanbag and be reduced to a state of catatonia by some mindless-American dysfunctional family-oriented sit-com? How many millions are still expecting *Dr Who* at 6 p.m.? This tragic Pavlovian response is the legacy of school. For many of us a great portion of our lives was spent listless in the labyrinth of those nauseous corridors. And, late in life, we can no more escape them than we could get out of PE with a letter written in our own blood.

The reason for this is the structure of the school day. School was neatly compartmentalised into hour-long segments, which could easily be subdivided into quarters or halves. This regime gave life an undeniable rhythm. A rhythm that found a divine correlation in the TV guide. The fact that school finished at 3.30 p.m. and by 4 p.m. children's programming was well under way seemed more than just mere coincidence. And, just as in school, the world of TV was based on hour and half-hour segments that that dovetailed beautifully to form entertainment. The repetitious nature of school suggested that the rest of life would be as seamless. When it wasn't, many of us fell apart.

I believe – and recent studies tend to support this thought – that the much-celebrated Australian laziness is due entirely to school. There are two ways to attack this dilemma. The first is to adapt our working hours to regular school hours. This would take the working week down to an easily manageable twenty-five hours a week (plus homework). The other option: to keep future generations of Australians in school a bit longer. It'd take a harmless piece of legislation to make the average school day from 8.30 a.m. to 6.30 p.m. That way, when the kids mature and have to hold down 'real' jobs they won't feel the urge to head home at 3 p.m.

This could also open up a new world for disenfranchised teachers. The payment of teachers in this country is appalling. Regardless of the fact that they educate and instruct our greatest assets they'd make a great deal more of the folding stuff in private enterprise. To get the wheels of industry turning again we need prim authority figures armed with pieces of chalk walking around our work stations forcing us to pay attention. If we're sluggish: a loving crack across the knuckles with a metal ruler. And, in my experience, nothing focuses the attention more than a blackboard duster hurled with ferocious intensity at the temples. Large corporations could employ these 'Matrons of Mathematics and Dukes of Discourse' to patrol offices, ready to confiscate tennis balls, rubber bands and pornography. Leaning on a shovel would be a thing of the past if council workers had Mrs Deportment, the third-grade English teacher who was only ever interested in posture, on their backs. But it's in the area of cleanliness that teachers excel. How spotless would our cities become if teachers followed around sanitary workers with that calm, commanding voice of authority, 'There's one you missed'?

For most of us, our conditioning became ingrained with a primary education. We emotionally begin each day at 9 a.m. and finish at 3 p.m., with bouts of imagined educational boredom in between. I pity the poor individuals (you may have them in your office or perhaps they're members of your family) who failed to progress to the secondary stage and remained fixated with a time-management program dictated to them in kindergarten. These are people who barely make it through the day without bursting into tears. They're normally a bit sleepy until 11 a.m., by 1.30 p.m. they're overexcited and experiencing rapid mood swings and by 2 p.m. they need a nap. At the sound of a piano they have an urge to lie down (which can make it difficult in a lift). After work they stand outside, looking maudlin, waiting for someone to pick them up.

The rhythm of school was beaten into us for eighteen years. Eighteen years in the mindless pursuit of knowledge. We moved from halls of mechanical precision into an organic world of chaos. Is it any wonder we're confused? Unless we act now the workers of the future will be the same. They'll sit at their work stations remembering play lunch: joyously swapping Pokemon cards, mimicking the Simpsons; and they'll wonder, from time to time, what ever happened to Dawson?[1] Just like us, they'll find themselves daydreaming at work, staring out a window, overcome with nostalgia for the great TV of the past and waiting. Waiting for that final bell to release them.

---

1.   When I ran the spell check over this piece the mighty machine queried 'Pokemon'. Its substitute word was 'Packman' (pacman). Nothing changes.

The Burden of the Old
School Tie

Describe what happened.
A couple of weeks ago I wrote a piece about the inescapable nature of school. It concerned the past, which continued to dominate the present. (That article was 'The Desire for the Old School Tie'.)

What makes this interesting?
The day after I submitted the article I received a fax stating that another article was part of the Year 12 curriculum. The students had to read and answer questions relating to an article that was reprinted for them. The article was mine ('Deconstructing Construction').

How did that make you feel?
Like the Education Department has sounded my death knell. I felt soiled, dirty. They used an article of mine as a test! I've become, through no fault of my own, a member of the establishment, assimilated into the school system, the thing that I despise.

Has there ever been a sadder moment in your life?
No.

Who do you blame?
I blame society, and the individual that thought it was a good idea. What kind of a world are we living in where our children are not only allowed to read this sort of crap but have to answer questions on it as well? Where's Proust, Eliot, Burroughs and Schulz? And, to my knowledge my permission was not sought. It leaves one to ponder the nature of the education system when literary theft is an accepted part of the curriculum. Who can answer honestly on a stolen document?

What was the article about?
It was about construction. The disturbing aspect for me is to talk of deconstruction and then to pose questions about the author's intent. This undermines the notion of deconstruction, where the interpretation of the text itself is of utmost importance. I would suggest that, unless the teachers are aware of what they're doing, this casual use of the term merely serves to confuse and muddy the already murky water of deconstructionism. It is even more fallacious in this instance, as part of the intent was to get through it as quickly as possible so that I could get to bed after a night of frivolity and excess, and nurse the hangover I knew was approaching. I now see it as my role to reconstruct the deconstructed construction.

What are your memories of school?
Gestetner, the scrape of chalk on blackboards, the misery of

friendship, the loss of faith, soured milk, Phil Hammond's scab collection and waiting – mainly waiting.

Were your years in school the best years of your life?
From my first cautious steps on linoleum floors in a demountable room that served as preschool, to that final run to freedom from a pebble-crete quadrangle at the end of Year 12, I could easily count them as some of my worst.

What can you do about it now?
I can attempt to subvert the course of education by offering the answers in a national newspaper. If any student has yet to hand in this assignment then I hope the notes of the author concerning the authored work may be of some assistance. (It also means the Education Department will be less likely to try this shit next year.) Here are the questions with my answers . . .

What is the purpose of the article?
Financial – purely a way of making money. There was certainly no depth to it or any artistic need to fulfil. I remember sitting at the Mac with two hours until a deadline and scribbling notes of annoyance – nothing more. In more civilised times I would have been called a whinger and that would've been it.

Comment on the effectiveness of the following.
What follow are three examples of the writer's work that for reasons of personal shame I felt unable to reprint. Suffice to say that they take a Victorian approach, meticulously overwrought and self-conscious.

What is the tone of the article?
Dull and aggressive.

How is the tone established?
By using too many adjectives and antonyms of words like beautiful, wondrous, picturesque.

What function does memory serve?
I can recall there wasn't much memory in it. I had succeeded in eating most of that away with that night of 'frivolity and excess'.

How does the writer make use of personal experience to present his views?
There was no personal experience. I haven't been out of the house for twenty years. I invented most of it and plagiarised the rest. In the real world you don't have to be good, you just have to be canny.

How effectively does the writer use the resources of language to engage the reader?
Not that effectively. On a scale of one to ten (where one is the love songs of Bread and ten is the work of Flaubert) I would say around three.

You might consider structure, vocabulary, mood and any other features you consider relevant.
Why consider – it's all there for you. Go outside and enjoy the day before they start taxing the air.

Any questions?

CONCERNING TELEVISION

Representations of Reality

The universe of carnage that spills from our TV sets reminds us of the fragility of life and how funny it can be if someone else cops it. Australia has embraced the recording of disasters since *Australia's Funniest Home Videos*. We laugh as a nation united if a child walks into a swing, bites the dog or punches an unsuspecting uncle in the testicles. Any accident, in or around the home, that's not recorded has become a complete waste of time. We've also discovered that if your clumsy kid is caught in the salivating jaw of the family pit bull you could be in for big money. But for many of us *Australia's Funniest* just doesn't do it any more. We've had to move on to something harder, something a bit later in the evening where the fun never stops: *When Animals Attack, What Went Wrong?, World's Wildest Police Videos, World's Funniest Natural Disasters, When Cows Explode.*[1]

Every night we're presented with a variety of gruesome choices as our post-dinner entertainment. The spectacle of 'reality' wins every time when pitted against Shirl repainting the pine. And *Getaway* seems so bourgeois when you can witness desperate human beings willing to overcome any obstacle in their bid to 'get away' to freedom. What can compare with that grainy out-of-focus shaky-cam video action? We all confront the same questions of taste. Although who can tear their eyes away: another oil tanker explodes, another fire in a New Delhi shopping mall, another bovine bomb.

It's contemptible, but for a spectator, a voyeur, it's damn engaging. The precarious moral subtext these shows use to justify the material is often more shocking than the footage. The reality is the camera lies and the cameras used on reality TV not only lie, they're unfaithful, fickle and a drain on your emotional resources. (This may be the reason reality TV is so popular – because it treats you like one of the family.) There will come a time in the not-too-distant future when we crave something harder. Have you noticed that a few too many people survive in the disasters? Where's all the stuff they are keeping from us? Where's the real 'real' TV? It hasn't made it to these shores yet but it's out there somewhere circling, waiting for its moment: *Death TV*.

Death TV makes *Australia's Funniest Home Videos* seem like the soul of discretion and propriety. The only positive thing about *Death TV* is, if you play it backwards, you might actually get a happy ending.

On *Death TV* people have had their video cameras on, loaded, focused and full of tape when calamity befell them. As tragedy struck they had the good sense to fire up the Sony. As family members experienced a hideous, yet visually exciting, demise, these documenters of domestic disaster were there with batteries to spare. Imagine being that lucky? And what good is that old videotape of Dad's unsuccessful parachute jump? It certainly doesn't make viewing the home movies much fun as he bounces on the desert floor like a house brick. But why should the nauseating tape gather dust when it could be sold and make Dad a posthumous star (albeit a falling one)? After all, he would've wanted it that way.

Are we ready for the husband encouraging his wife to video him as he communes with nature? Tragically he communed with a seven-foot grizzly bear that with one swipe of its paw removed his head. The loyal wife continued to film, her hand frozen in disbelief. Her husband's body slumped lifeless in the national park as a Not-So-Gentle Ben went off in search of honey.

Surely a headless man riding a bicycle is funny? And surely it's social satire when the newlyweds drive into the back of a cement mixer? And surely it's ironic when the exploding cow's intestines hit the protesting vegetarian in the mouth?

These are the wonders that await us when we take that inevitable step into the abyss of taste. It's good to know the world is currently obsessed with observation. Every day more and more surveillance cameras are put in place. We delude ourselves that this is for our own protection, when we know in our hearts its prime function is for entertainment. These cameras are working tirelessly to bring us the accidents, crimes and great comedy moments of the future. As another parachute fails to open, our families will be brought closer together through someone else's sadness. We'll all continue to enjoy reality TV as long as the reality isn't ours. Isn't it about time we made *Death TV* a natural part of life?

---

1.   An exciting big-budget avenue no-one has explored yet is the combination of reality TV and popular sit-com characters. For instance: the

cast of *Friends* are in a life-and-death situation inside a burning shopping mall in New Delhi as David Hasselhof rides an exploding cow on a sinking oil tanker. Who will survive? Stay tuned.

In Praise of TV

We entered this new century obsessed with change. This obsession is mirrored in every aspect of our lives but has found its truest reflection in television. It's the reason programs like *Backyard Blitz*, *Changing Rooms*, *Hot Property*, *Ground Force* and *Better Homes and Gardens* are so popular. On the surface they present easy, entertaining ways of improving our living spaces but the subtext of these shows is one of dissatisfaction – dissatisfaction with our homes, our yards, our furnishings, our holidays, even our pets. Nothing makes us happy any more (apart from the slim chance that a TV crew and a troupe of burly aesthetes might tramp dirt through our house and save us from our own bad taste).

The question is: why do we continue to delude ourselves our rumpus rooms and backyards are the problem? This frantic desire for domestic improvement may well be disguising the real issue. It's all well and good to paint over the cracks and rip up the underlay but at the end of the day, when we look in the Tonia-Todmanised mirror, we come face to face with what we can't escape. Jung suggested the home represented the unconscious self. Bachelard believed various rooms within a home depicted different aspects of our nature. Why waste time with 24-hour revamps of property when we should be renovating ourselves? The logical extension of this current trend in TV would be to take unsuspecting members of the public (offered up for televisual consumption by concerned family, friends or business partners) and radically alter *them*. The technology is available, and with a few clauses to prevent lawsuits, we could be away.

Channel 7, 8.00 p.m. *Jodie thinks she's a frump. In twenty-four hours we'll transform Jodie-the-dour-old-frump into Jodie-the-Supermodel. Impossible? Come with us as we find out. It starts at Jodie's birthday party. Won't she be surprised when she discovers the party is just a ruse to 'knock her out'? Once she's 'away with the fairies' we'll take her to Australia's finest cosmetic surgeon for some much-needed rhinoplasty. When we achieve the button-nose she's always wanted, we'll swap wards to rip that unsightly fat out of her inner thighs and buttocks with some high-powered lipo-suction. We have two new breasts from our good friends at Dow Corning. And as a special bonus, to give her those Formula One racing curves, we'll remove two floating ribs. When she wakes up she won't be able to recognise herself.*

If you think people are surprised when they see the change to their backyards imagine their shock after a head-to-toe total body makeover. It'd be like watching a car crash, backwards, in slow motion. And why end it there? What about a show that physically transforms women into men and vice versa. Many people feel uncomfortable with their gender but don't have the massive finances needed for that most delicate of operations. The money would be a doddle for a TV company. There'd be kickbacks from airlines, hotels and product placement, not to mention experimental pharmaceuticals from the chemical giants and scads of free scalpels. Another bonus – the production company could easily rush through the time-consuming psych. reports and hide any damaging evaluations. It's a win–win situation for everyone involved.

Channel 9, 10.00 p.m. *You may remember Jodie. She was uncomfortable with her beautiful new body and face. After extensive grief counselling our psychiatrists found the answer – she's a man trapped in a woman's body. It's now our job to get him out. Jodie has agreed to let us fly her to Mexico, one of the world's most polluted cities, where she'll be pampered before being placed in a coma. We then travel by bus to Tijuana, the black-market-plastic-surgery-Mecca, for a heavy-duty overhaul. It's here, at a secret location, that she'll enjoy all the wonders of gender reassignment. Be there to see her ribs come home.*

Combine this personal version of *Backyard Blitz* with *Love Rules* and you'll have a hit.

Channel 10, 11.30 p.m. *Lara is a thirty-five-year-old mother of two with her own plumbing company. She's desperately seeking true love and an honest relationship. We've decided to team her up with our most recent success story – Hank. Hank has gone from strength to strength after returning from Tijuana. Lara is totally unaware that Hank used to be a woman. Our hidden cameras will reveal the fun and games. And, who knows, if we're lucky we could see good ol' Jodie taking Hank Jr for a test run.*

And on the other stations?

SBS, 9.30 p.m. TVTV. *A squad of Hungarian footballers hang up their boots in favour of Crimplene slacks and hit the town. Meanwhile Olga is having trouble deciding which side to dress on.*

ABC, 12.05 p.m. *A sensitive documentary about a couple who fell in love on a TV show. Hank thought he knew everything about Lara. But the one thing he didn't know, and the one thing the production company didn't tell him, is that his new wife used to be a man.*

Schools of Cinema

This is an old story. It comes from a time when minuscule art-house cinemas did battle for the lowly Aussie dollar against a tireless army of Hollywood giants. In those days I was a staunch advocate of European films and I loathed America's cultural emptiness, its overpaid actors and bloated sense of self-importance. These two schools of cinema were ideologically opposed. Where one was dark and brooding the other was light and fluffy. Where one left you with a mass of unanswered questions the other answered all your questions – even the ones you didn't think to ask. Where one went well with popcorn and soda the other required a bowl of borsch, a raw turnip and the patience of a saint. Where one ended neatly at an altar with a young couple vowing undying love, the other ended in a confusion of surreal images: an armless mother is laid to rest as hirsute dwarves juggle the intestines of a white stallion while cobbled streets are washed down with a big ol' bucket of cow's blood. The End.

They were worlds apart – as were the people who went to see them. On fortunate evenings when the art-house cinema finished at the same time as the cinema of frippery the two groups would meet and ascend the stairs. Ours, dressed in fashionably faded black, faces set like stone, trudged solemnly out of another largely ignored Fassbinder classic. Our post-picture conversation was littered with uncertainty: *Who's Maria Braun? What did it all mean? That was great, but I wonder if anyone could tell me if I enjoyed it?*

Meanwhile the opposition, faces beaming, would stride happily out of the cinema. They would dance on the stairs and swing from the banisters. They couldn't control themselves and occasionally broke into spontaneous song. They had no questions. What was there to question? They made statements: *That was brilliant, Dustin Hoffman was great as a woman, that Macaulay kid is going to be big.* And when they returned home, they made love for hours fuelled by the memory of their big-budget American film experience. We, on the other hand, seldom made it home. With the themes of horror and estrangement fresh in our minds we'd retire to coffee shops to dissect and disseminate: *It was so German but somehow universal at the same time. It spoke to us all – in another language. Even though it was set in Holland in the 1640s and everyone wore wigs, something about it reminded me of Queanbeyan.*

I was happy in that world of angst, blissfully unaware it was about to change. Unaware my redemption was at hand. It was a cool Melbourne night and myself and two companions were at a loss for something to do. We had scanned the cinema listings and the dark and dire fodder that was our favourite fare was nowhere to be seen. Instead a banquet of banality was stretched out before us – wall to wall American pap. Unable to make a decision I washed my hands of the situation and left it to my friends. It was bad enough agreeing to see one of these offensively expensive and shallow films without being implicated in its selection.

The film they chose was *Back to the Future* and it was showing at a kitsch monument to excess called The Forum.[1] I kicked and screamed on the way in but I left elated. I had been saved by *Back to the Future*. Michael J. Fox (who many considered at the time to be the Antichrist) led me into the light. He rescued me from the long, bleak corridors of European cinema, from Tarkovsky's spiritual landscapes and Herzog's examinations of human suffering. And in their place he filled me with happy-go-lucky-gosh-gee-willickers-wonder. Since then I have never looked back, taking every opportunity to indulge my passion for crap. My friends abandoned me, preferring to focus on Kieslowski festivals – seeing *Dekalog* instead of *Doc Holiday*. They say I've gone to the dark side, but I know I walk in the light. It's not for me to judge. I believe everyone has their own *Back to the Future*. I'm just grateful I'll never have to sit through foreign credits again earnestly appreciating names I can't even pronounce.

---

1. Shortly after my filmic Damascus The Forum become a place of worship (perhaps the spirit was already moving in it) where a Christian outreach group performed musical plays every Sunday night. The interior of the venue housed a number of classical statues. The new proprietors considered them offensive but because they were part of a National Trust building they couldn't be moved. It was strange to witness Charismatic Christian ceremonies surrounded by naked Greek and Roman figures but it gave the room a joyous pagan warmth. One could imagine, after

a round of praying in tongues and a bit of interpretation, someone would be sacrificed to 'Jasper, the horn'd god of fun' and a bacchanalian orgy would commence. Thankfully, in a room packed with corduroyed Christians, it never happened.

Concerning the Self

CONCERNING THE SELF

Entropy

• Part 1

[the art of self-destruction]

I 'm sitting in a dark room. The room does have a light in it, like every other room in this place. There's no reason why this light shouldn't work apart from the fact that it's *my* light and it's in *my* room. I'm the reason the light doesn't function.

I first read about the unnatural order of things in the *Presbyterian Ladies' Handbook of 1906*. Four years later I was able to cross-reference the rather graphic material there with a chapter in *Happy Homemakers; A Religious Guide to Modern Living* from 1872. It wasn't until recently, with the publication of *The American Journal of Interpersonal Relationships* (June 1999), that I was able to correlate the information held in the other two books, information that suggests that everything is not as it appears.

It's often been asserted that we influence our surroundings by our moods. But to suggest this has a physical effect on the world has always been a matter of some dispute. Just as certain people radiate joy, there are those who radiate something else. We're all in a state of entropy but some of us are degrading more rapidly than others. We may even be degrading others. We destroy things. The much loved *human touch* is fiercely corrosive.

The sweat and weight of our hands can smooth marble or polish brass. We've seen the damage our grubby acidic hands do every time we touch each other or ourselves. But there are some who have this effect on their environment without the need of touch. They may do it through words or ideas, and sometimes even their mere presence makes things spoil. The *Ladies' Handbook* demonstrates this beautifully by listing three different types of people in the world.

1. The first group comprises the 'peacemakers'. They appear in our lives as little bubbles of bright energy. Swarming with life-affirming platitudes, sporting cute button noses, and screamingly sincere, they skip along the street arm in arm with wonder. These people create harmony wherever they go and their mere presence brings a sense of peace. It's important to note they're relatively scarce.

2. The second group is where the bulk of humanity resides. Homer Simpson is revered as the archetype and worshipped in some circles as a god. Here people are content, addicted to chocolate or alcoholic pacifiers and joyously inert.

3. In the third section there are those who, through no fault of their own, have a tendency to break things.

I belong in the last category. It's been a long, hard journey to get me to this realisation. I have pondered it, questioned it, examined it, and there is no other explanation. The common denominator in the wanton destruction that takes place around me is me. I am the epicentre of menace, the focal point of failure, the ultimate waste. I have finally accepted the fact that when an object is placed in close proximity to me it will age more rapidly, expire, corrode, self-destruct or have an emotional episode. It doesn't seem to make much difference what it is: vegetable, animal or mineral, everything falls apart around me. Food will spoil, jams will sour and farm machinery will fail in its function. Silver becomes tarnished, gold turns to lead, watchbands putrefy on my wrist. Computers break down when I touch them. Toasters explode into dazzlingly surreal displays of light. Animals seek any avenue of escape to get away from me. On occasion, when I have been stationary, domesticated beasts have urinated liberally on my lower limbs to display their disgust with me.

To discover where you belong there's an easy test: keep a freshly opened carton of milk nearby as you work. If the milk, within half an hour of exposure to you, sours or begins to form a putrid skin, seek help. (For your own peace of mind try this on a cold day.) If you can't find any milk try asking yourself the following questions. Is your TV's remote held together with sticky tape? Does your mobile phone still have an aerial? Do you have a seemingly insurmountable problem with unwanted body hair? Do you think open fires are infinitely more fascinating than human beings? Do you ever drive by sense of feel? Have you ever been mistaken for other members of your family by your parents? Do you have two bags permanently packed and ready to leave beneath your eyes? Do you ever think reindeer are dispensable animals? Why can't you be bothered finding the milk? Do you work for Telstra?

If you answered yes to any of the above it's probable you belong in the final category. This is nothing to be ashamed of. We're the bacteria of social interaction. We break the mulch of society down into fertiliser. We're as essential as negativity.

Without us, people would have nothing to compare their happiness to. So even if you're a total failure, a black hole of abject misery, don't be concerned, for you fulfil an important role in the grand scheme of unnatural things.

Entropy

• Part 2

[the body of evidence]

I t's begun to soften in its old age. It's begun to accumulate creature comforts. Gone is the back-breaking cotton-wadding spirituality of the futon, replaced by the life-replenishing inner spring. Gone is the search for adventure, replaced by lethargy and contentment. Gone are the late-night alcohol-fuelled descents into greasy culinary disaster, replaced by a need to find foods that don't cause heartburn, bloat or gout. Gone too are great chunks of memory. At the end of a ludicrously long day at work it needs to throw itself down on a recliner rocker. It wants a private foot spa. It longs to be massaged with fragrant oils. It desires fresh clothes and store-bought shoes. It wants to bathe in the glow of the cathode ray and fall asleep with its slippers on.

My body has begun to betray me. It happens to all of us who live long enough. There are pains in my joints that never used to be there. My meagre muscles feel like over-stretched elastic. I've begun to sag. I'm losing the interminably slow battle against gravity. There's a wax build-up in my ears that could provide the raw materials for a lucrative candle business. My body is covered with countless freckles. It's only a matter of time until one of them shows its true colours and admits an allegiance to the sun. The only thing I can look forward to in old age is bifocals. I've discovered I need to scrub my teeth with something approaching an interest in oral hygiene. It's no longer effective to run a brush across the rancid pegs or rinse with a splash of contaminated tap water. There are other smells, things I dare not mention, things that remain a private moment between myself and my medical practitioner. I can say this: the bone machine that has served me so well for so long, without ever complaining, has begun to complain. The entrances (or exits, depending on your point of view) of my body have begun to need attention. They itch for attention, they ache for attention, they dribble, splutter, ooze for attention. They require a soothing balm, a touch of ointment. Once they performed their various necessary, if off-putting, functions with a minimum of maintenance. Now, after years of abuse, they're reacting with something resembling resentment. There is something else, but I can't put my finger on it. Not because I can't explain it – I'm just terrified of infection.

Another terrifying aspect of this perversely slow rate of decay is that I've begun to realise how important a chemist is. As a younger man there was only ever one reason to visit the pharmacy of fun. Now I hang at the counter with the other 'survivors of youth', the vitality challenged, script at the ready. I envy them: at least their afternoons are filled with the heart-threatening action of bowls. I remain in the store letting my hand trail along shelves of Spirulina and Metamucil. I crave antihistamines. I wonder what I'm missing out on with Ponstan. I've found a temporary home between the corn pads and the sports bandages and I can loiter in front of the vitamin racks for hours.

I'm divided: my mind and body have begun to squabble. My

body keeps trying to convince me that lawn bowls is a terrific way of meeting people. It maintains that the all-white outfits worn at competitions are a pretty good look. When I try to rationalise with it, my body won't stand it. It has no concept of common sense and why should it? In the overpowering realm of the heart's hysteria how pathetic is the rational? But my mind, belligerent monstrosity that it is, keeps trying.

My body has responded to this by allowing dark black hairs to sprout from my ears and nostrils. They're like a dense foliage of twisted vines annoyingly seeking the light. They're primarily the reason for these feelings of decomposition. I was stopped by a proudly fawning couple in the street recently. The reason for their happiness was the *Vogue* fashion plate five-year-old they'd created together. I leant forward to examine the fruit of their loins as his prying fingers found my nose. He tugged at some loose hairs and exclaimed that I was 'a wombat, an old man wombat'. His parents were deliriously overjoyed with this observation while all I could remember was the old saying, 'Out of the mouths of babes comes half-digested food and dribble.' I allowed the five-year-old his moment in the sun because I knew something he didn't. It comes to us all in time. We're built to self-destruct, to wind down slowly, to corrode. The human body, this marvel of creation, the pinnacle of earthly perfection, has one fatal design flaw. So laugh while you may, spoiled designer-label-leather-jacket'd child. I forced a smile, my yellow-grey teeth inches from his chubby cherubic face. And I allowed my rancid, ancient, anchovy-loving breath to cover him as I wheezed, 'They're cute when they're that age.'

The Creature from the

Back Room

I t was one of three photographs of myself my family had dragged out. Although a number of years separated the photographs I was wearing the same school uniform in all of them, which gave them an unnerving unity. In the first one I was about eight and was smiling straight into the camera. I looked so happy, I found it hard to recognise myself. The same face beamed from the next photo taken three years later. Then there was the third photograph, the one when I was around twelve, the one that instantly made everybody laugh. In between the giggling fits someone managed to spit out, 'What on earth happened?'

Within a moment the way I viewed myself stopped, my development ceased and a single negative image became fixed in time. This reference point burnt out all that preceded it and all that would follow it. It's often difficult to find where the instant began. I am luckier than most – I have a photograph to remind me.

It was undeniable that something had changed in those few years. It was more than bad lighting and a poor subject – my entire demeanour had altered: my eyes were downcast, the heavy metal spectacles I wore appeared to cut into my nose, my mouth had curled into a sneer, my hair had darkened to a lank and greasy mop. I had become 'the thing'.

As my family pointed and laughed I remembered what it was like to be thirteen (because that seemed to happen a lot when I was thirteen). And I knew something they didn't: the way I look in that photograph is the way I see myself today.

That version of me – the thin-lipped myopic monster, the human toad, the creature from the back of the room – is the one I cannot erase. It's installed in my visual memory and no amount of you-beaut feel-good positivity can dislodge it. We can spend a lifetime trying to escape those awkward adolescent moments but they lurk in the subconscious until conditions are ripe for them to return.

For me it lifts itself out of my psyche like a teenage Mr Hyde running quietly amok in my life. I'll be at a dinner party and there sitting in my seat is that gangly acne-ridden mouse-haired invertebrate. I wonder why the other guests have said nothing. I wonder how long I can get away with it before someone throws me out. I feel like a great pretender waiting nervously to be uncovered. My outward appearance has not changed but inwardly I am thirteen again and I find myself picking the scab off an emotional scar. I find I am too frightened to speak, nervous and embarrassed, and any confidence I have has evaporated. I tell myself: it doesn't matter what's outside, it's what's inside that counts. And what's inside is a throwback, a mutation, a stunted nondescript. Then as mysteriously as it appeared 'the thing' has gone.

The only saving grace is I'm not alone. There are some of us out there who have magnified one second of weakness for the duration of our lives: the girl who tucked her skirt into her undies, the boy who sees himself with a Marella jube eternally stuck in his braces, the one who wet their pants just before the bell went, the slowest, the shortest. It could relate to a piece of jewellery, a pair of shoes, a shameful incident, and it waits to be reborn. There is a girl I know who was the tallest girl in school and some days she still is the tallest girl in school.

Do people in positions of power confront these demons or are they forced to live with them as well? Does Clinton picture himself as a clumsy, sexually illiterate youth when he speaks to Congress? Does Tony Blair recall miming to Beatles songs in his bedroom with a hairbrush? Is Howard the epic knight, the Queen's colours tied to his lance, tearing another blanket from a Hills Hoist windmill? Do their alter egos ever rise up in moments of crisis and 'go the spoil'? Is there any way of overcoming this stumbling block?

I tried for a while to replace the negative image with a positive one but nothing worked. I looked for things I could be proud of, I searched for any triumph or success – perhaps if I had won something, achieved something, if I could find something positive. It was a useless exercise – nothing I compared it to had the same power. I had to concede the weakness was victorious.

I can see the boundaries of my life, my limitations, the structures that enclose and surround me as clearly as the border of that photograph. As my mother slipped the photo into a frame and placed it on her sideboard I couldn't help feeling he had won again. Even as I write he has been here. Crouching at my shoulder, whispering in my ear, grateful that I have given him shape.

The Belief in Superstition

Recently a friend of mine purchased a second-hand car. Justifiably proud of the new acquisition, he pointed out the many splendid features of the 'deluxe' model from '71: the vanity mirror, the padded sun-visor, the personal flow-through airconditioning. He was incredibly lucky to find it, the second car he looked at; what a bargain. He mentioned it was owned by a little old lady who only took it out to get the shopping once a week. As proof of this doubtful tale he pointed to the St Christopher medal on the dash. It was a black disc about an inch in diameter. A painting of a hooded figure complete with staff sat in the middle of the disc surrounded by opal shavings. It was an authentic small protective magnet and it sat slightly out of view beside the steering wheel. I remember his saying, 'It's quite a good little St Chris,' as he pried the medallion off the dashboard to give me a better look. I only had the medal in my hand a second, just long enough to notice the image had yellowed with age, before we ran into a safety wall.

If one was superstitious one might make a connection between the taking of the medallion from its resting place and the subsequent smash. Certainly this was the view of the owner, who now has several clustered over the dashboard of his newest car. The tragedy also made him an instant believer, a crusader for Christ and a more cautious driver. Although the cards were stacked against me I couldn't help thinking it was nothing more than a coincidence. I cannot recall seeing anywhere that St Christopher has to remain on the dash or swing from the rear-vision mirror to be effective. Is the tiny safety officer off duty when he is in your hand? I thought Ol' Chris had failed in his function because, in point of fact, he was still in the car.

There will be numerous times in the course of your life when you will be forced to make a decision between coincidence and an event preordained by destiny. No matter how extreme the circumstances I have always sided with the haphazard nature of nature. But sometimes even with all the will in the world it is hard to prevail against the undeniable truth of a situation.

One such incident occurred in London several years ago when I was working in theatre. One of my fellow performers mentioned, while we were backstage preparing for a show, that earlier in the day he'd tried to avoid a black cat. He hadn't succeeded. The damn pesky critter had managed to get in front of him and, with malicious intent, had crossed his path. He not only assigned intelligence to the beast but also an awareness of the myth regarding the awesome power it possessed. I was amazed that a mature, educated adult could place any faith in an 'old wives' tale'. A heated discussion ensued where I wilfully walked under a ladder, smashed a small mirror and performed numerous other feats of stupidity to prove nothing would happen: the world would not shift on its axis, there'd be no plague of frogs, no tsunami from the sink would engulf us.

My companions refused to agree with me; their response was simple: 'You wait.'

I decided to throw down the gauntlet. I shouted the name of the Scottish play. Those versed in the folklore will understand this is the ultimate test of the theatre gods. To say the name *Macbeth* backstage is anathema. The tragedy is said to be cursed and the mere utterance of the word will bring down the wrath of whatever powers that be upon the poor players: death, destruction, loss of income, failure to reproduce and every other evil imaginable. In some circles even to think of it is considered dangerous. But to run around half-naked, screaming it out in a variety of ludicrous voices while pretending to be Isadora Duncan, Richard III and a Womble is an insult to every sensibility – akin to throwing a pressed ham at the Almighty.

My friends informed me I had flirted with fate and the very heavens would be set against us. Their threats of imminent devastation failed to impress me. I took to the stage fearlessly while they followed with some trepidation. Needless to say the night was splendid, the audience was warm and responsive, the show an unqualified triumph. We came off stage and drank three pints of bitter to the fables of the theatre. Four days later the guitarist broke his arm, the company lost thousands of pounds on cancelled shows, and we returned to Australia in disgrace.

Fortune, fate, circumstance, coincidence were not blamed for these incidents – I was. To this day I maintain my innocence. It had nothing to do with me. It was not the mocking of *Macbeth*, the walking under the ladder or the smashing of the mirror that had caused these tragedies, it was one thing and one thing only – that damnable black cat.

The Survival of the Fittest

I've had the symptoms for years: stomach cramps, lethargy, questionable moral judgement; but it was gratifying finally to be able to point the finger and blame something – Sydney water.[1] Without the TV bulletins, newspapers and radios constantly warning us I wouldn't have realised that the water was toxic. Even after being repeatedly warned I still woke up the next morning, rolled out of bed, and poured a bacteria-laden glass of tap water down my throat. As the crisis subsided I was conscious that in any other age I probably wouldn't have survived. I wouldn't have lasted two minutes in the bush, the jungle, the desert or any other natural environment. As a member of this species I may have been dragged to the top of the evolutionary ladder but I'm barely hanging onto the bottom rung. I'm a creature designed for sofas, a human beanbag. I couldn't run if my life depended on it. Thankfully, the late 20th century protects people like me – it nurtures us and provides an environment where we may flourish. Any other age would have flushed us down the toilet.[2]

Darwin's theory of evolution, which incorporates the notion of the 'survival of the fittest', has given way to the 'durability of the dumb' and the 'endurance of the awkward'. Our predators are few and far between but we are beset by other dangers that must be overcome. So what if our waterhole was poisoned? It is a sad indication of our times: our greatest threat is decay.

Here's an example.

The other morning I decided I'd have crumpets for breakfast. It was a decadent thing to do in the current climate of financial uncertainty, but I threw caution to the wind. I was moderately proud of the spread, a simple banquet: the crumpets were hot, straight from the toaster, and I managed to time it so the tea wasn't tepid. A friend arrived unexpectedly and I invited them to share my breakfast. My hunger got the better of me and I hoed in, but it all went horribly wrong when I offered my guest the other crumpet and they declined. Their refusal, unerringly polite, still managed to annoy me. The upset I felt had more to do with my own insecurity than their lack of appetite. Were they allergic to crumpet? Not hungry? Had they eaten already? I had to know.

They told me they found the pale blue mould off-putting.

I hadn't noticed any mould. They drew my attention to the discoloured patches covering the remaining crumpet and if I concentrated hard enough I could actually see some. The longer I stared the more definite the mildew became. A little hairy forest of fungus filling every pit and hollow of the crumpet. I am not a very observant person – nothing to be alarmed at – but occasionally I miss subtle things like mould. (This being said I had noticed they hadn't touched their tea – apparently the milk had curdled and great creamy curds floated all around the top of the Irish Breakfast.)

I hadn't noticed the fluffy pale blue mould; however, this didn't trouble me as much as the fact that I hadn't tasted it. So not only am I colour-deficient, but I also have a very unrefined palate – a peasant's palate. The sort of gob that could devour mountains of rancid 'tatties and 'nips and wash it all down with a bucket of mucus. I'd die hours later of a burst intestine or ruptured spleen and never even know why, but I'd probably have enjoyed the feast while it lasted. In the animal kingdom nature warns the unaware when something is dangerous to eat – mould growing off a carcass is an obvious one. You'd have to be one dumb carnivore not to notice it. The stench of death must be everywhere in my kitchen and I can't even smell it.

Over the years the world has become a safer place for people who are hazardous to their own health, those of us who, left to our own devices, would clumsily throw off this mortal coil and blunder into oblivion. Our instinct for self-preservation has been reduced to turning off the tap and even then most of us couldn't get it right. We have survived through sheer weight of numbers – there are more of us than them. We form a protective coating around each other and propagate. We admire the fit from a distance and mock their calorie-controlled lives, their obsessive natures, their determination. As we hobble along with walking sticks, short-sighted, colour-blind, deaf, with dry, damaged hair and an endless supply of mood-altering pills it's becoming increasingly apparent it's not only the fittest who survive, even the weakest are doing very well. There is one last word of caution – watch the water.

---

1. See 'The Olympics' (p. 88) and 'The Unseen Dangers of Water' (p. 150).

2. Not every other age had a 'flushing' toilet as we know it; I refer here to any device used for the disposal of waste.

The Phlegm Baby

Please do not read this if you are easily offended by sickness and its often bizarre ramifications.

I have of late been gripped by the fear that I will not make it to another spring. The reason for this notion is that for six months I have been stupidly battling the same cold. I'm certain it began sometime last summer. I have a lot of phlegm on my chest, more of it every day, and there is nothing I can do to get rid of it. I am filling up internally with mucus, I make a sloshing sound whenever I walk, a sea of slobber is lapping in my lungs. I had accepted it as part of my life, an unnecessary, upsetting part of my life, or at least I had until I came to 'the understanding'.

I have been able to cope with the extra strain this flu has placed on my body; what I have not coped with is the mental and emotional strain. My fears have taken the form of daydreams, nightmares and musings about what could be happening with my cold. The other day all the madness dissipated and a clear blue and brilliant day emerged from the chaos.

The cold was growing inside me, feeding off me, and that's

when the revelation occurred. I've had this virus for over six months: that puts me at the end of my second trimester. As absurd and deluded as it may sound, hope surged in my heart – just twelve more weeks and it would all be over. After nine intolerable months of flu I'll finally give birth to a seven-pound bouncing ball of phlegm. A phlegm baby, a child composed entirely of snot and mucus, fruit of my lungs, custard-apple of my eye, a spit off the ol' block.

I don't know how it happened, these things go around, it's not like I was careless. There must have been something in the air that day. I remember everyone was sneezing, not even bothering to cover up. I walked right into the thick of it. I didn't care, we were young and everyone was doing it. Still, when I realised my body was changing it was too late to say I should have had protection, a nasal spray or some sort of pill.

You have to nurture a phlegm baby by really watching your diet – nothing nutritious can pass your lips. You can't have fruit and vegetables, or echinacea, or antibiotics – any of these things could kill the baby or, worse, stunt its growth. You have to smoke constantly. You have to drink whenever you're not smoking. You have to avoid handkerchiefs and tissues. You have to work extralong hours, consume thickshakes, avoid the sun, stay in bed, watch *Oprah*. If you do all these things you'll give birth to a healthy hunk of nose floss. I'm a little worried because I didn't realise what was going on until quite late in the gestation. I'm concerned I may have eaten something decent in the preceding six months. That's why I have to go in for an ultrasound to see if everything is normal. Just to check and make sure my spawn has a creamy complexion, not too green or too yellow, not too lumpy, not too smooth. See if the little one has all its fingers and toes.

I have thought a lot about the impending birth. Will I need drugs for the pain? An epidural? Should I go for a natural birth or Caesarean section? Should I go all hippie and hunker down in the flotation tank? There are so many questions and all the medical fraternity I've approached seem reluctant to discuss it with me. The Caesar concerns me, purely on the vanity level.[1] I'm aware it's unusual, something out of the ordinary; I'm certainly not as young as I used to be. But just because I'm a bit older that's no reason to be treated like a freak. I can suffer the indignation for now and the whispered comments and the stares because it won't be long before I hatch my little clotted gummi-bear, my sticky-pudding cherub, my soft-succulent-snot-nosed kid.

When that day comes I'll push my glutinous fledgling along in a stroller, another lone parent struggling with my offspring, and the only thing that will swell in my chest will be pride. People will stop me in the street, peer at the product of my nasal cavity and exclaim, 'Oh how cute, he's got your cold.'

---

1. The visual imagery that would usually accompany this comment is so grotesque that I have decided to withhold it. However, if you are in an experimental frame of mind you may conjure up your own. The publisher and I take no responsibility for the infection of the body or mind that results from this piece.

The Pursuit of Solitude

The television is throwing a warm ethereal light across the room. I have drawn a blanket up to my throat and I'm in a dressing gown, yet despite these precautions I'm cold. The marrow in my bones is frozen. I made a decision over this long weekend to set myself apart, to distance myself from the world, to find solace in solitude, to question, meditate and thus come to a deeper understanding of life – but I bore quickly and the TV is an easy distraction.

Thousands of feet above the ground a man walks along a thin bar from one balloon to another; a Frenchman, without a cage, swims across the Atlantic; a young Australian woman swims from America to Cuba; millionaires are constantly floating around the world in an attempt to imitate fiction. Men and women, but mainly men, decide to pit themselves against the elements in an ongoing battle against themselves and nature. They are running solo through wastelands, deserts, across treacherous frozen expanses and mountainous terrain. If they achieve their goal they become a hero, if they fail in their task and are found alive they become a survivor. Either way they win, and if they die, they become another footnote to the limits of human endurance.

Every time I turn on the box, there is some idiot going solo. In the world of today the physicality of the body has taken precedence over the abstraction of the mind – to the point where mental pursuits are totally overpowered by the physical prowess of sporting fanatics. There are so many that the TV can hardly contain them. They come bursting out of the screen at the end of every newscast as a sort of fantastic and humorous conclusion to the day's events accompanied by a knowing laugh from the presenter, 'Ha, ha, ha and in Holland a man has buried himself and his dogs in a statement about world famine, next.'

Yet the solo pursuit is no longer a solo pursuit. It is covered by every available media outlet: keypads are whirling, books are being published. The only thing waiting at the other end of the journey is a possible tele-movie on some rat-shit American cable channel. *My Struggle with K2, How I Conquered the Antarctic, Sixty Days at Sea Clinging to a Sweater*, The Loneliness of the Long Distance Runner, Swimmer, Pole-vaulter: it never ends. There are film crews, agents, paratroopers on a rescue mission and some kid who survived four days face down in the snow on nothing but frozen rabbit droppings and Mars Bars; TV crews are documenting another extraordinarily dumb tale of survival.

Every day someone is coming out of the ocean or going into the desert. They're going it alone, with a major sponsorship deal, a coach, a dietitian, a support network of thousands and occasionally a higher goal: 'I'm crawling through the Serengeti on my knees for world peace.'

Traditionally these periods of isolation were linked with some kind of spiritual, emotionally or intellectual growth. Philosophers once set themselves apart from the masses: they climbed to the top of a snow-covered peak, crawled into a cave or wandered into the desert. Descartes, the famous philosopher, no longer able to bear the cold and wearing only his dressing gown, clambered into his stove. He stayed there and meditated. When he came out, his fundamental principle of life – 'I think, therefore I am' – was finished. Descartes gave privilege to the mind over the body. He denounced bodily senses as deceptive and maintained that it was only through the mind that we were capable of reaching certainty: he found his reason by sticking his head in an oven.[1] Did the TV crews and papers celebrate his emergence from the stove? 'René's out of the stove, and he's got something in his hand. It looks like, it is, it's his philosophy.'

Remember Tony Bullimore? He was nothing more than a polyp successfully removed from the tortured colon of Mother Earth. When millions of dollars had been spent, and hundreds of hours searching, what revelation did he impart to us? Did he gain some new insight huddled in the hull of his upturned yacht? Did he achieve a different perspective on the world? – 'I wanna do it again.' And like Tony, when all the others are pulled from the wreckage of their planes, yachts, hot-air balloons or bicycles suffering exhaustion, frostbite, dehydration and barely strong enough to knock on death's door, the reason for their journey is inevitably the same: they wanted to prove it could be done. To which the logical response is, 'It can't.'

---

1.   Don't try this at home. Not everyone who crawls inside an oven will

come to a greater understanding of themselves or humanity. The world is littered with those who have tried to emulate Descartes's journey of self-realisation only to realise the gas was on. Sylvia Plath is just one example.

The Brandy of the Damned

Preface to the Piece

This is a gripe from an old man, a tirade of abuse that is totally
 unjustified.[1]

The Piece

Every day there's more of them. Like a harmonically sound,
generically attractive Paterson's curse, they're spreading across
the earth killing everything in their path. Thriving on a diet of
fairy-floss love, and sprouting quicker than nasal-hair on an octo-
genarian; they're high on life, fuelled by innocence and bank-
rolled by jaded advertising executives with sinus problems. Every
nation has a squad of identical individuals in duos, trios, quartets
and quintets (never exceed six). They're the sanitised messengers
of Satan, Rosemary's babies of music all grown up. They're the
phenomenon known as the boy/girl groups: interchangeable,
undeniable, ever-present.

Our notions of contemporary beauty are established by these
groups' promotion and design departments. Our children look
like bonsai versions of their karaoke heroes. They are mirrored

Concerning the Self

by thousands of munchkins who swoon to the sickly sweet syrup of songs. In the most depressed countries in the world, there are tonally challenged, monophonic troupes working on their dance steps. Even our own 'backwater of civilisation' boasts a few copy-cat acts testing out the funky moves with the smooth multi-layered vocal tracks. In all these songs 'love' floats mindlessly in happy-happy land on fluffy pink clouds. If this sonically brain-washed generation ever confront the less tasteful physical aspects of love they'll be justifiably horrified.

Where did they begin? Stories abound about the origin of the same-sex vocal groups – who may or may not be able to sing. Some blame The Monkees, but there's a big argument for The Jacksons or their antimatter nemesis The Osmonds, or we could lay the blame with The Andrews Sisters or The Supremes, or Bananarama. But at least these groups had some level of talent and could sing in harmony (with the exception of Bananarama). For my money the responsibility lies with Milli Vanilli, for it was with these two bovine, tone-deaf Euro-trash models that musical ability became completely divergent from music. Milli Vanilli had neither style nor substance, but they did have a producer, a video, and impressive miming skills. Mime – a dead art form reborn in the mid-seventies to become a prerequisite for a career in music. The swarthy German lads, who sang in English but couldn't speak it, made it abundantly clear that talent should never be a hindrance. They were thought to be attractive (obviously by the record producer, who had never stepped out of a studio) and visual acceptability became a matter of course. Prior to Milli the saleability of an act was not totally reliant on smooth skin, come-hither looks and a passable box-step.

The fledgling groups come in two handy-to-market genders

– male and female. Producers of these fast-growing, unit-shifting monstrosities learnt early on that it's a definite mistake to mix and match. All it would take would be one post-pubescent descent into depression on an over-long tour for careers and credibility (note the ironic tone) to be ruined. Singing about love all the time and never getting any could play havoc with the adolescent mind, and proximity does make the heart grow rational. In these circumstances, when the ex-rock-pig-chaperone was comatose on Bundy rum our mixed-up starlets would take a quick trip to heaven – and all hell would break loose. We need only look at ABBA to see the sadness that cross-fertilisation can cause. When the group terminated they'd attempted every possible combination of partners without success. Now like any reasonable ex-couple of couples they no longer speak to each other except through their lawyers.[2]

Despite all the savagery, the boy/girl groups have given me a reason to live. I want to stagnate to a ripe old age. I want to be there when they wheel out a 150-year-old Oprah. I want to hear her say, 'Ever wonder what happened to the New Kids on the Block? Take That? Spice Girls? Boyzone? All Saints? Five?' Ad nauseam. I want to be there as the Goss brothers (back together for the first time in fifty years) ask again when they will be famous. I want to record on my archaic VCR the *Ricki Lake Show* that begins, 'I was a member of a multimillion-dollar boy/girl group but I now perform demeaning sexual acts for a pittance and no-one even remembers my name.' And maybe then, and only then, I will believe there is a god.

1.   I am probably bitter because I like that new Spice Girls song and I hate myself for it.

2. This is a complete fabrication. I have no idea how the retired members
    of the Swedish super group relate to each other and I really couldn't
    give an ounce of highly toxic, acidic faece.[3]

3. I was perturbed to discover that this term only comes to us in the
    plural – faeces – which I found singularly offensive.

The Remembrance of Perfection

I have searched this world over and never found it again. Occasionally, like a face long forgotten, it appears in a crowd, surfaces for a second, and disappears. I thought I caught a whiff of it in Morocco once: in desperation I followed a decaying series of passageways to a sweltering market, where in the mix of exotic spices and animal droppings I lost it.

We all have smells that awaken buried memories. These odours are personal and individualistic and have a significance which is all their own. Smell can provoke memories more powerful and all-encompassing than any others: it's when the olfactory receptors and the much-maligned nose prove their worth – with a single sniff, they cause the head and heart to swim with an overwhelming rush of nostalgia.

The smell I picked up on that street and lost was the acrid artificial fragrance of a transparent plastic bag. A bag I bought from a corner shop for a pittance when I was seven. A bag that contained little green American WWII soldiers. A smell I have searched for in vain all my life.

As a child I gnawed on any object I could get my fluoride-enhanced, calcium-deprived pegs around. All manner of toys,[1] plants and furniture suffered at the hands of my teeth. I spent many an idyllic afternoon licking lead or gnawing on aluminium saucepans. But that all changed when I purchased *the bag*. I'd been attracted to the pack because of the graphic cardboard seal depicting the D-day landing with liberal splashes of blood and death and, of course, the strong smell emanating from it. The stench was so artificial, so fake, so disagreeable, it scented the entire store with the odour of cheapness.

At home, in the privacy of my room, I ripped off the cardboard and a powerful charge of aromas enveloped my head. From that second I was lost. The plastic of the bag had fumigated and permeated the soldiers. Each one carried a hint of that special pong. I couldn't resist and chewed on the muzzle of an M16. Before long I had attacked the entire platoon. A leg here, an arm there, a tiny radio pack. Limbs hung loosely on tendons of stringy green plastic, snipers lost their heads, foot soldiers were unable to stand after I ate their pedestals: it was carnage. The army that had emerged whole and fragrant was reduced to a dirty dozen ragtag lepers.[2] I needed more.

When I returned to the corner shop they were all sold out. No doubt word had spread like wildfire among the juvenile hedonists in the area. All that remained on the rack were crappy Sherman tanks, amphibious vehicles, and vanity sets moulded in a hard, unforgiving synthetic. I have reason to believe that the special plastic I loved has since been banned. Banned by some nameless international convention governing the safety of small children. I have little doubt it was poisonous and yet I would give almost anything to find it again. No smell has come close to the wonder of that bag. It was the most moving odour I have ever experienced and evokes the utopian experience of childhood. No food or beverage that's passed my lips has matched the intensity of that plastic. I can only suspect it is akin to the sensual pleasures the ancients derived from the pomegranate. Over the years I've searched. I have stood in toy shops sniffing the air – I once ate a relative's Christmas present – but it's never been the same. To this day, the slightest suggestion of that smell magically transports me to a time of innocence.

How fortunate we are to live in this age of the artificial, this time of plastic – not because of the multitude of uses, but the smell. How many generations have gone to the grave without experiencing the intoxicating odour of rubber on a hot day? How dull the scent of lavender when compared to latex. How many children have been forced to chew the ends of sticks never knowing the untold joys of chewing the heads off little green plastic American soldiers? Was there ever a product that was so good to put in your mouth and so stupid to swallow?

---

1. It is best not to use toy soldiers, or indeed toys of any kind, as a dietary supplement.

2. I realised, later in life, that the injustice I'd inflicted upon my men depicted, visually, the true horrors of war. The happy-go-lucky gun-toting group of healthy-minded whole-limbed infantry were replaced by gnarled stumps of spittle-ridden plastic. But unlike society I chose not to remember the brave ones who'd fought for my freedom. I left them forgotten and discarded at the back of a drawer to gather dust. There were no ticker-tape parades, no welfare, no support. Eventually they were buried in an unmarked shoe box, in a shallow grave, beneath a house brick.

Concerning the Concern

I have become a blight, an abscess, a problem. Some people have been reading between the lines of these weekly columns and found 'mental delirium combined with themes of grandeur' in the writing. The smattering of letters I receive are preoccupied with one thing and one thing only:[1] my mental stability. I am, I'm told, unhinged. Thankfully the writers of these letters have been kind enough to include the names of good psychiatrists (good in the professional, not the moral, sense). Some of these 'pleas for commitment' have been sent by psychiatrists themselves spotting a touch of manic depressive psychosis in the articles. (Perhaps business has been poor and they've been forced to solicit.) They maintain that their primary concern is for my wellbeing. They fear for my sanity, my unfortunate yet imminent demise, the mess I'll make when I hit rock bottom.

I've never felt so cared for by people I don't know. It reminds me of the Spanish Inquisition where the great love the interrogators showed their subjects often resulted in death.[2]

In response to concerns about my 'negativity' or, as one carer put it, 'the underlying text of suicidal tendencies', I have to say that I have never desired to do away with myself. It's true others have wished to get rid of me, but like an unwanted guest at life's party I've hung on in there. Those who know me think of me as a fun-loving, free-wheeling sprite of a people person, at ease with myself and in the company of strangers. My nickname of Mr Grumpy, The No-Fun Guy and Weirdo are only used in jest. Still these calls for my institutionalisation have occurred regularly throughout my life.

As a youngster I was a timid and uncertain thing, in outlook essentially jolly but prone to fits of melancholy. To combat this I was fond of drawing, and at any opportunity I would sketch. The ideas were childish and I am guilty, to this day, of the same introspection. I found the rectangles of white paper doorways to other worlds. Worlds of skeletal figures dancing in putrid fires, of bulbous-headed children with monstrous, searching hands, of hairless creatures hollowed and inhabited by nightmares.[3]

My sister, who was justifiably proud of her brother's strange creations, asked if she could exhibit them for 'show and tell'. We were twelve at the time. I was filled with pride and overcome with doubt. I was proud she thought so much of my humble doodles and yet I hesitated: this would be the first time my drawings would leave the safety of the family. The first time that I could be scrutinised by other eyes. I eventually agreed, and as the folio of sketches left my room I felt an immediate sense of loss. I didn't have to wait long for judgement. The next night my sister, in tears, told me that the nun's response was unequivocal: the drawings amounted to pornography and were the product of a sick and unhealthy mind. They should be destroyed – burning would be best. It would be advisable if I sought out medical help and my sister was remiss in her role as a family member if she didn't inform my parents of the sad and sorry state of their eldest boy.[4]

At ten, there were the Christians who saw me dancing and claimed I was the manifestation of a monkey, at fifteen, the Mormons who woke me too early one Sunday morning and received a brutal, if lacklustre, monologue on the dangers of sleep deprivation. They returned to bless the house once a week and cast out the demon. They succeeded when I left the home. At seventeen, a fellow student, hearing a poem I had written read anonymously by a teacher, called for my castration. At nineteen, a health inspector claimed I was slaughtering animals for fun and profit in my backyard.

It continues to this day. In these columns I was attempting to offer an antidote to the standard fare of the Sunday papers, an alternative to the ceaseless parades of tasty cuisine, carefree holidays and rampant materialism. I have failed. I attempted to suggest that the society we live in is diseased; you have responded by telling me it's I who am sick. And yet some good has come out of all this: I now realise how troubled I am and without your help I might never have noticed. Over the years numerous people have requested that I see a 'doctor' and I have always wondered whether it was for my health or theirs. I have always resisted the siren call of institutionalised sanity, but these days I'm just mad enough to do it. I promise I'll go tomorrow.[5]

---

1. This is false. There are numerous letters that congratulate the writer. McDermott focuses on the negative, he lies and then needs to confess. He speaks here in the third person, using a different voice, which would indicate schizophrenia.

2. Does this comparison suggest a massive persecution complex or is it mere paranoia?
3. Suggests hallucinatory experiences with grossly abnormal antisocial behaviour.
4. Delusions of grandeur combined with a poverty of thought from an early age.
5. Transparent attempt to win favour by accepting the diagnosis. I doubt there'll be any discernible change (e.g. tomorrow never comes).